# GRIMMY™
### Inc.

# Mailmen
# Can't Jump

## by Mike Peters

**TOR®**

A TOM DOHERTY ASSOCIATES BOOK
NEW YORK

*To David Williams...a dog's best friend.*

This is a work of fiction. All the characters and events portrayed in this book are either products of the author's imagination or are used fictitiously.

GRIMMY™: MAILMEN CAN'T JUMP

www.grimmy.com

This book contains material previously published in a trade edition as *Grimmy: King of the Heap.*

A Tor Book
Published by Tom Doherty Associates, LLC
175 Fifth Avenue
New York, NY 10010

www.tor.com

Tor® is a registered trademark of Tom Doherty Associates, LLC.

ISBN: 0-812-57460-5

First edition: February 1997
First mass market edition: September 1999

Printed in the United States of America

0  9  8  7  6  5  4  3  2  1

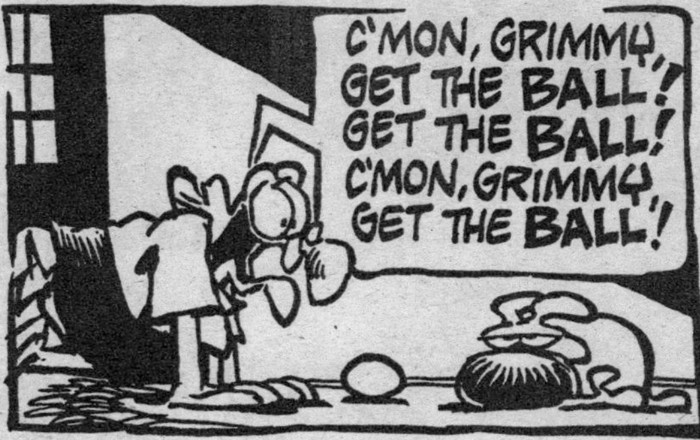
C'MON, GRIMMY, GET THE BALL! GET THE BALL! C'MON, GRIMMY, GET THE BALL!

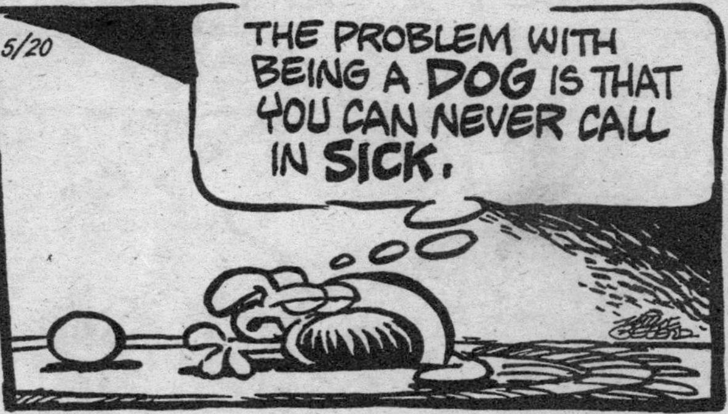
5/20
THE PROBLEM WITH BEING A DOG IS THAT YOU CAN NEVER CALL IN SICK.

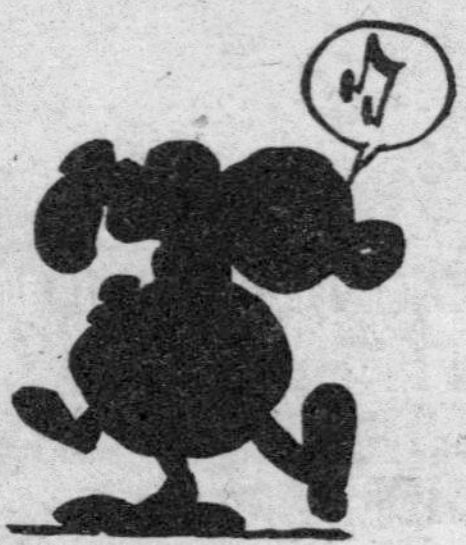

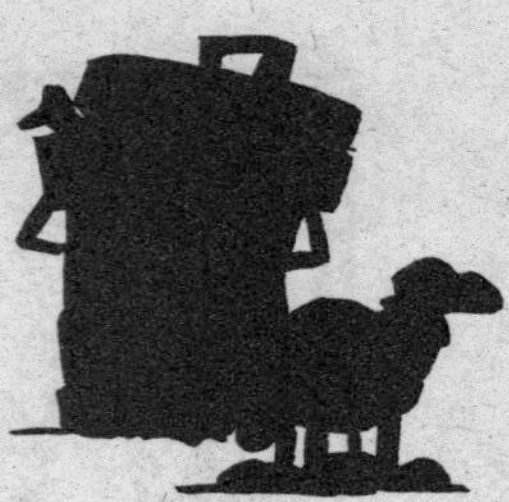

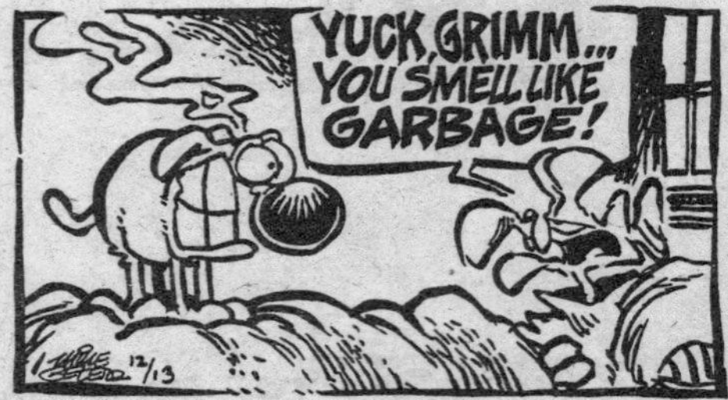
YUCK, GRIMM... YOU SMELL LIKE GARBAGE!

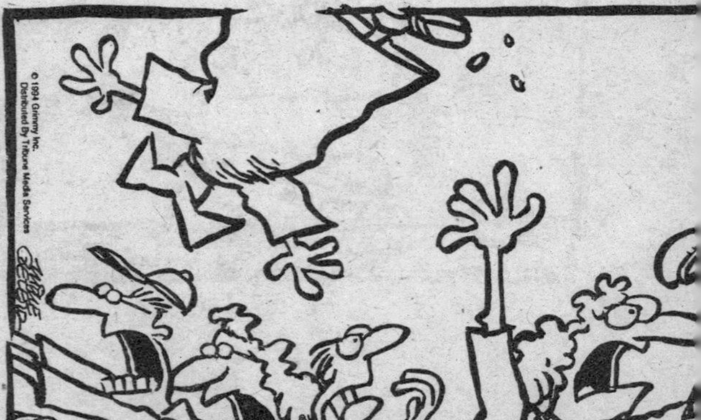
© 1994 Grimmy Inc.
Distributed By Tribune Media Services

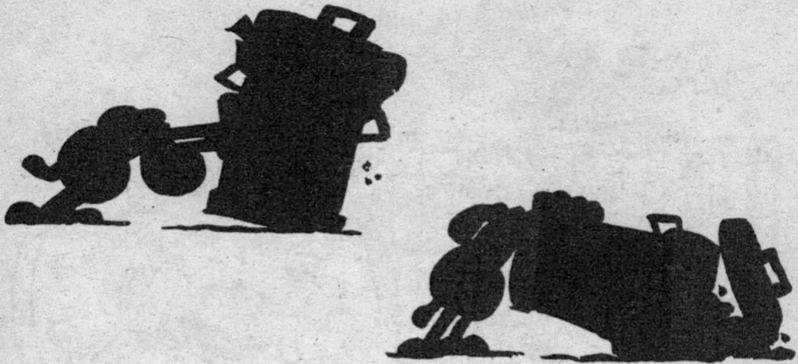

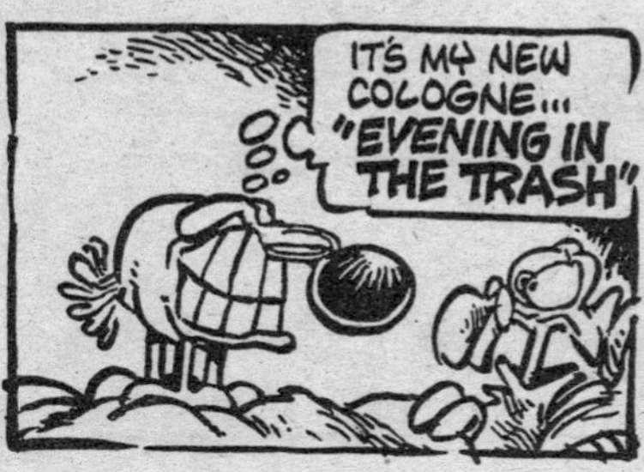
IT'S MY NEW COLOGNE... "EVENING IN THE TRASH"

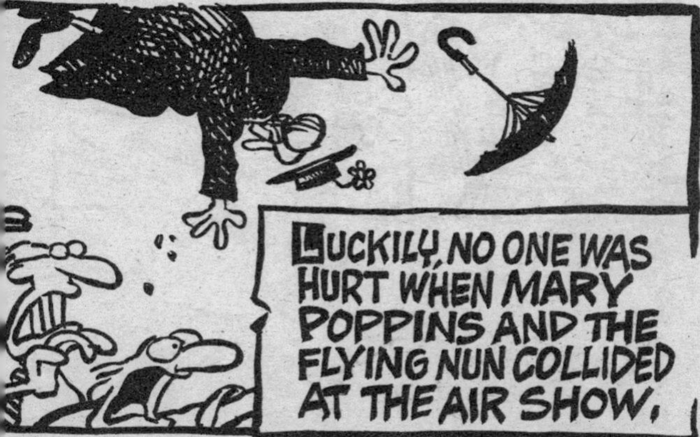
LUCKILY, NO ONE WAS HURT WHEN MARY POPPINS AND THE FLYING NUN COLLIDED AT THE AIR SHOW.

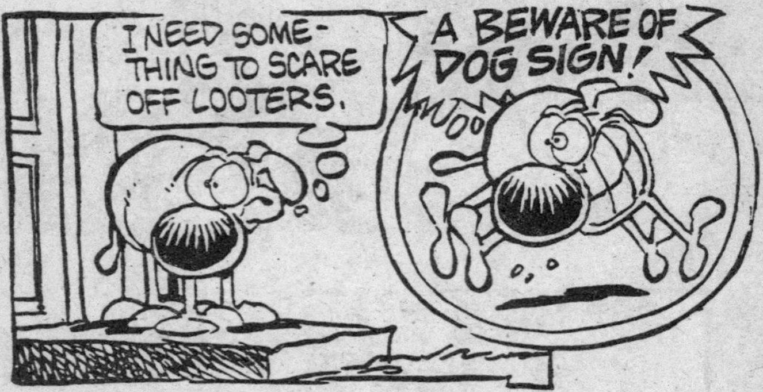
I NEED SOME-THING TO SCARE OFF LOOTERS.
A BEWARE OF DOG SIGN!

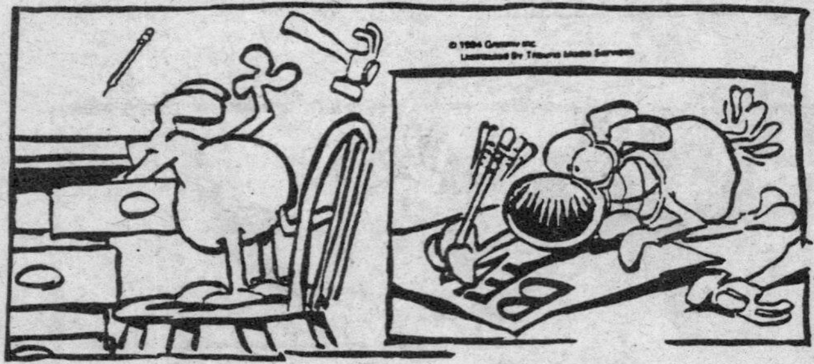

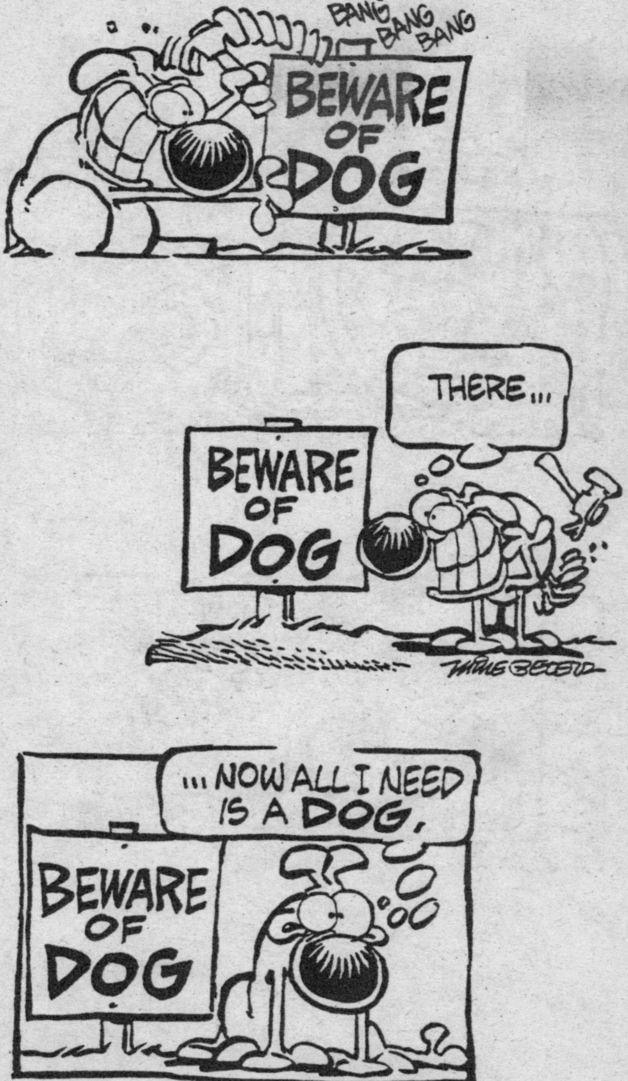
BANG
BANG
BANG
BEWARE OF DOG
BEWARE OF DOG
THERE...
BEWARE OF DOG
...NOW ALL I NEED IS A DOG.

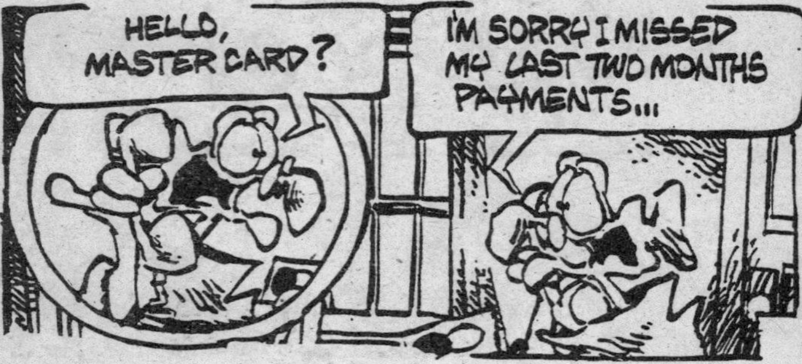
HELLO, MASTER CARD?
I'M SORRY I MISSED MY LAST TWO MONTHS PAYMENTS...

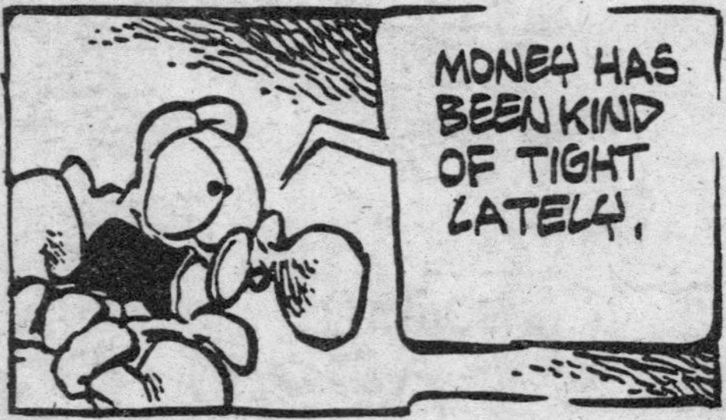
MONEY HAS BEEN KIND OF TIGHT LATELY.

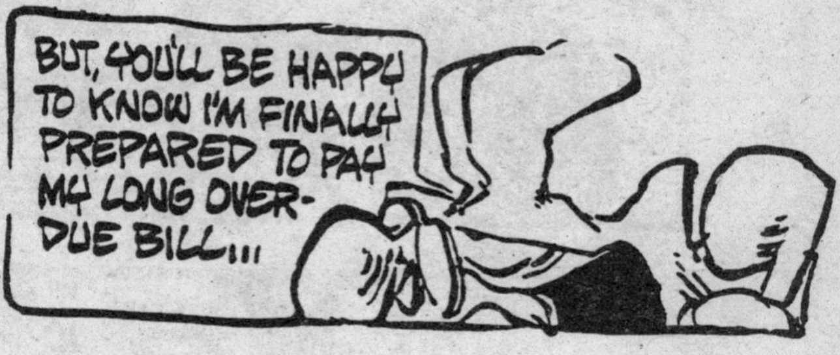
BUT, YOU'LL BE HAPPY TO KNOW I'M FINALLY PREPARED TO PAY MY LONG OVER-DUE BILL...

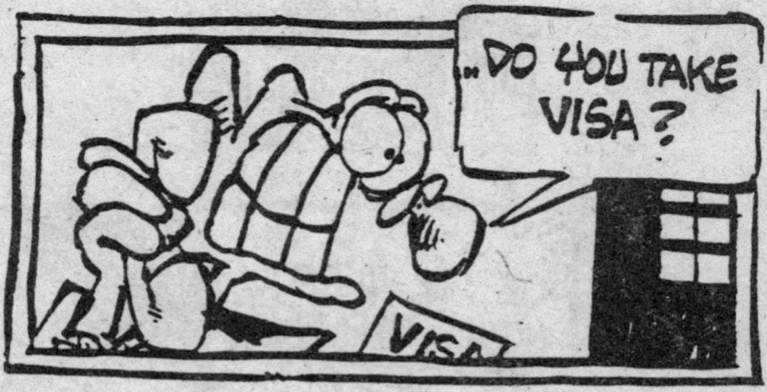
..DO YOU TAKE VISA?
VISA

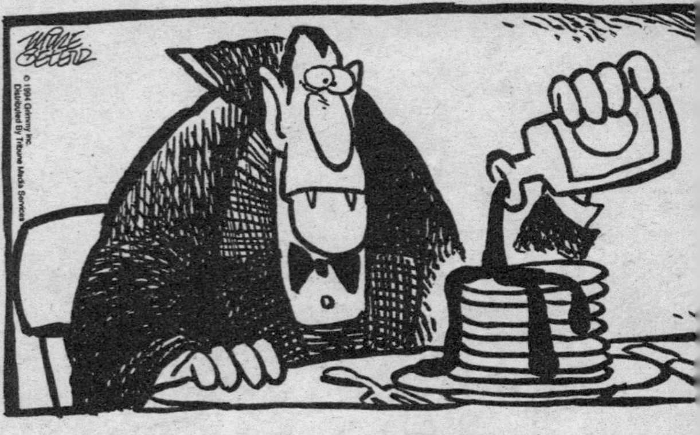
© 1994 Grimmy Inc.
Distributed By Tribune Media Services

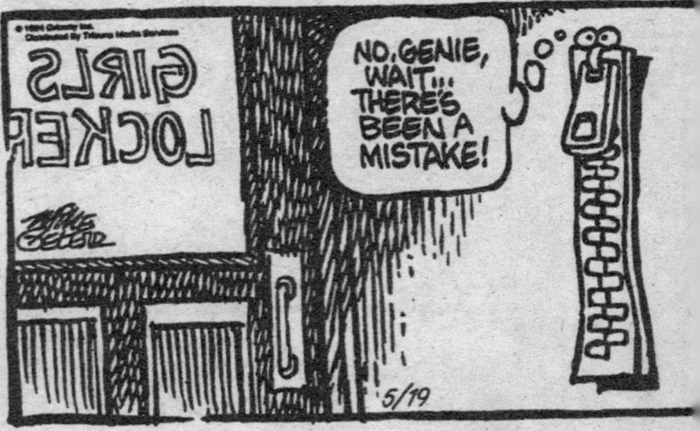
GIRLS LOCKER
NO, GENIE, WAIT... THERE'S BEEN A MISTAKE!
5/19

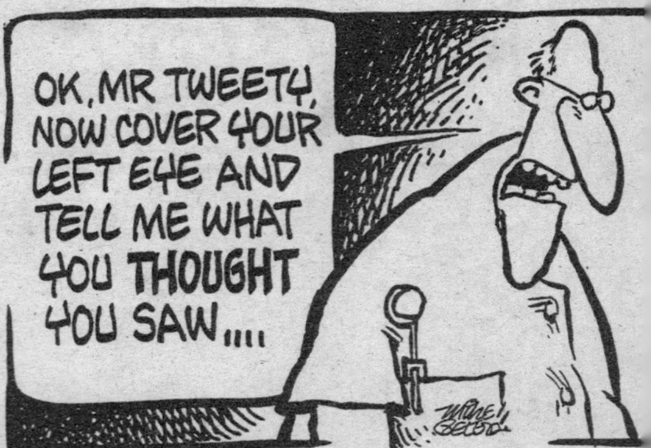
OK, MR TWEETY, NOW COVER YOUR LEFT EYE AND TELL ME WHAT YOU **THOUGHT** YOU SAW....

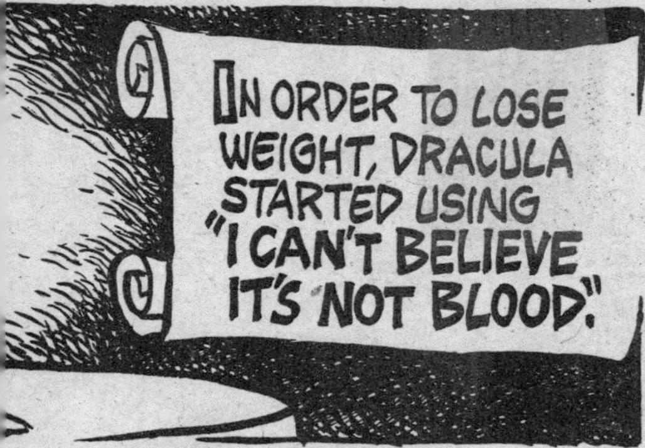
IN ORDER TO LOSE WEIGHT, DRACULA STARTED USING "I CAN'T BELIEVE IT'S NOT BLOOD."

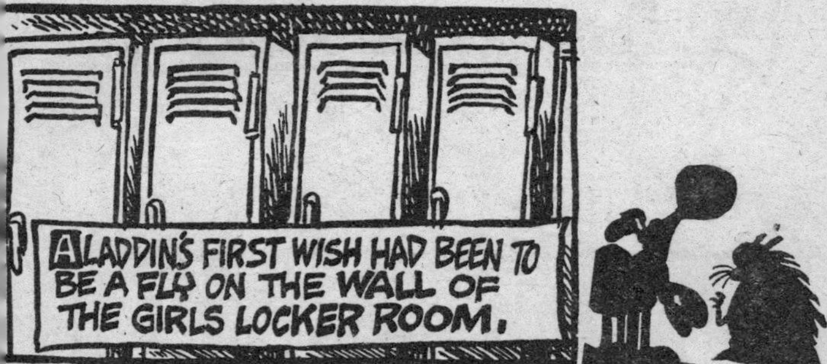
ALADDIN'S FIRST WISH HAD BEEN TO BE A FLY ON THE WALL OF THE GIRLS LOCKER ROOM.

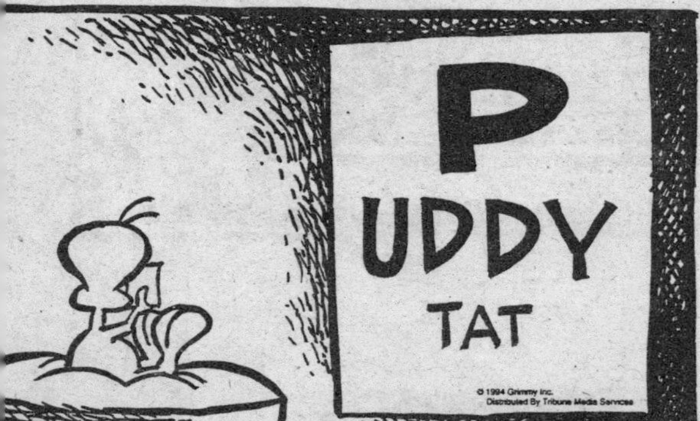
P
UDDY
TAT
© 1994 Grimmy Inc.
Distributed By Tribune Media Services

YOU'RE A SICK, DISGUSTING, VULGAR LITTLE DOG AND I WANT YOU TO SIT SOMEWHERE ELSE.
5/16

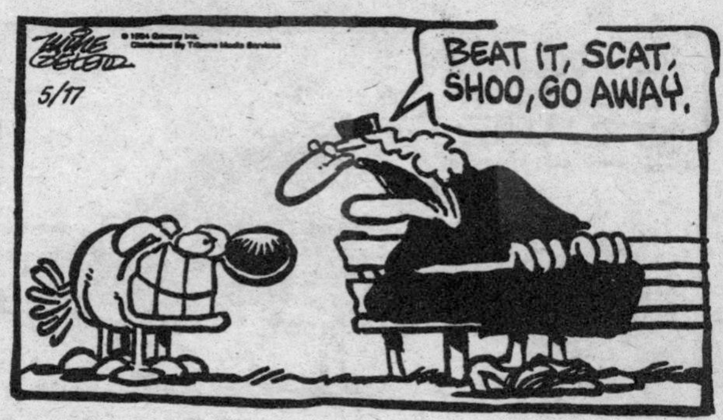
5/17
BEAT IT, SCAT, SHOO, GO AWAY.

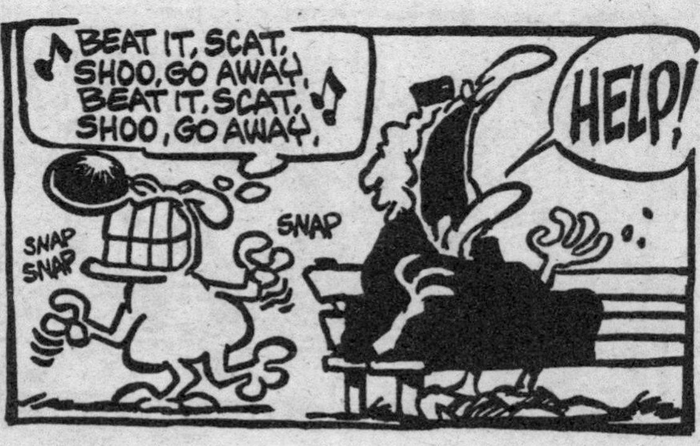
BEAT IT, SCAT, SHOO, GO AWAY. BEAT IT, SCAT, SHOO, GO AWAY.
HELP!
SNAP SNAP
SNAP

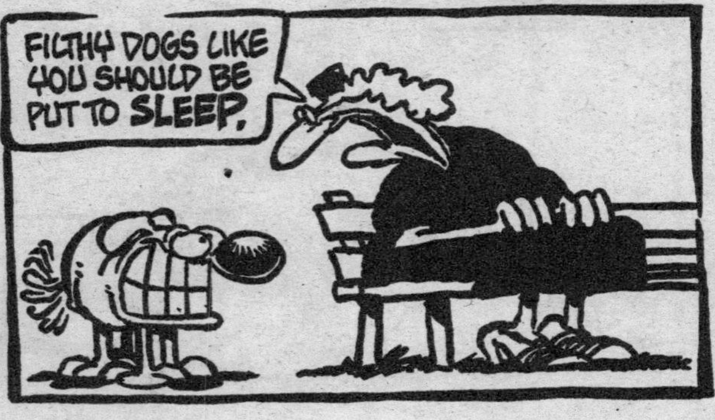
FILTHY DOGS LIKE YOU SHOULD BE PUT TO **SLEEP**.

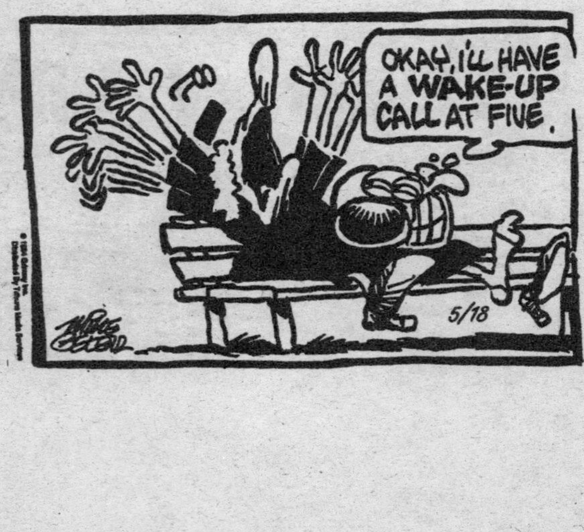
OKAY, I'LL HAVE A **WAKE-UP** CALL AT FIVE.
5/18

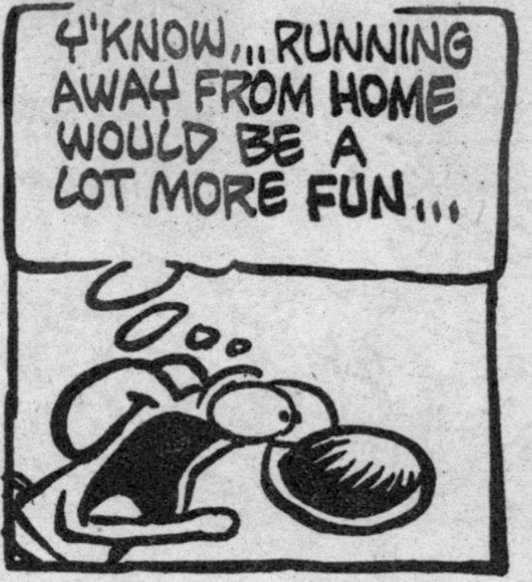
Y'KNOW... RUNNING AWAY FROM HOME WOULD BE A LOT MORE FUN...

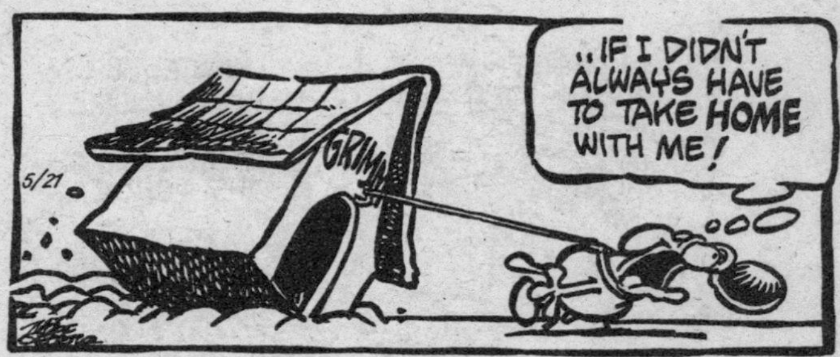
..IF I DIDN'T ALWAYS HAVE TO TAKE HOME WITH ME!
GRIMM
5/21

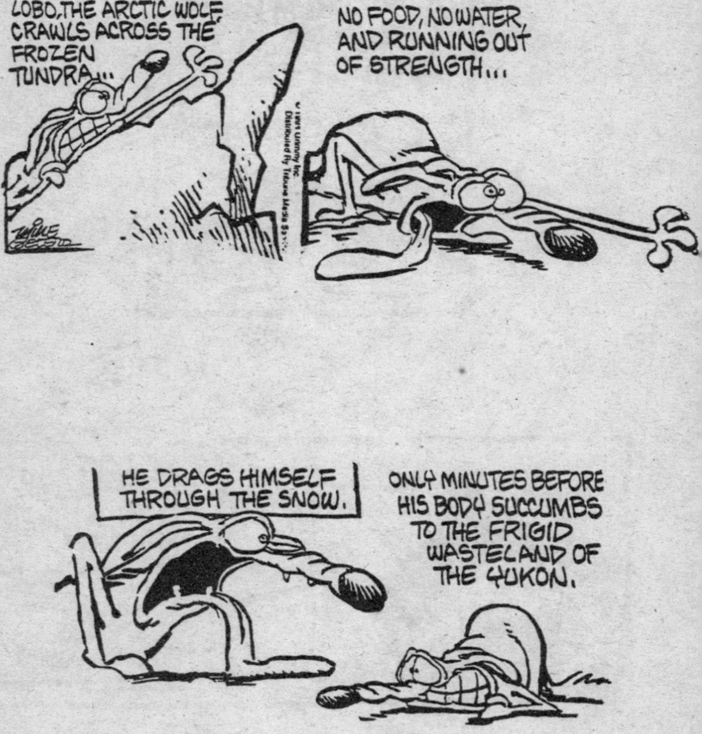
LOBO, THE ARCTIC WOLF, CRAWLS ACROSS THE FROZEN TUNDRA...
NO FOOD, NO WATER, AND RUNNING OUT OF STRENGTH...
HE DRAGS HIMSELF THROUGH THE SNOW.
ONLY MINUTES BEFORE HIS BODY SUCCUMBS TO THE FRIGID WASTELAND OF THE YUKON.

MIRACULOUSLY HE SEES A SOURCE OF WATER...

WITH EVERY OUNCE OF STRENGTH, HE STICKS HIS TONGUE OUT TO REACH IT.

THUDDENLY LOBO'S TONGUE GETH THTUCK ON A FROTHEN FIRE PLUG

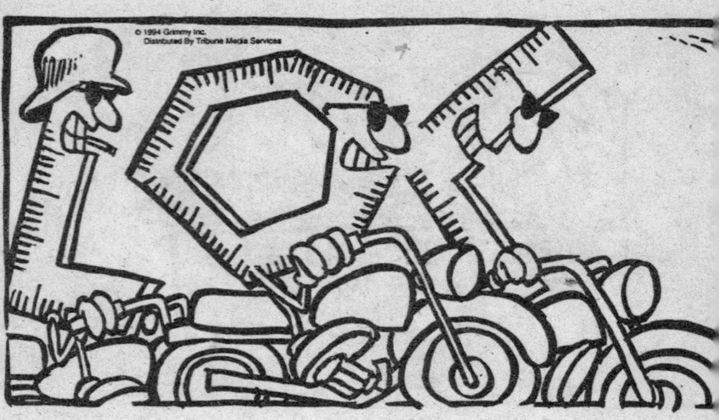
© 1994 Grimmy Inc.
Distributed By Tribune Media Services

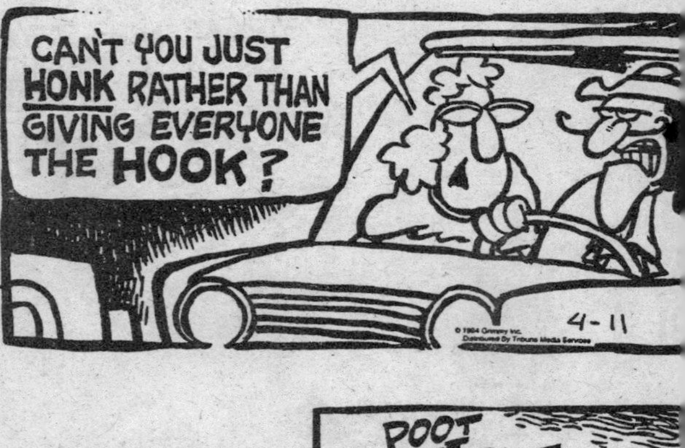
CAN'T YOU JUST HONK RATHER THAN GIVING EVERYONE THE HOOK?
4-11
© 1994 Grimmy Inc.
Distributed By Tribune Media Services

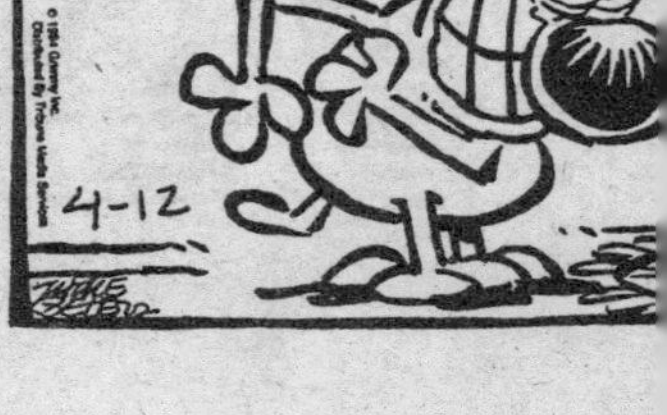
POOT
POOT
POOT
POOT
© 1994 Grimmy Inc.
Distributed By Tribune Media Services
4-12

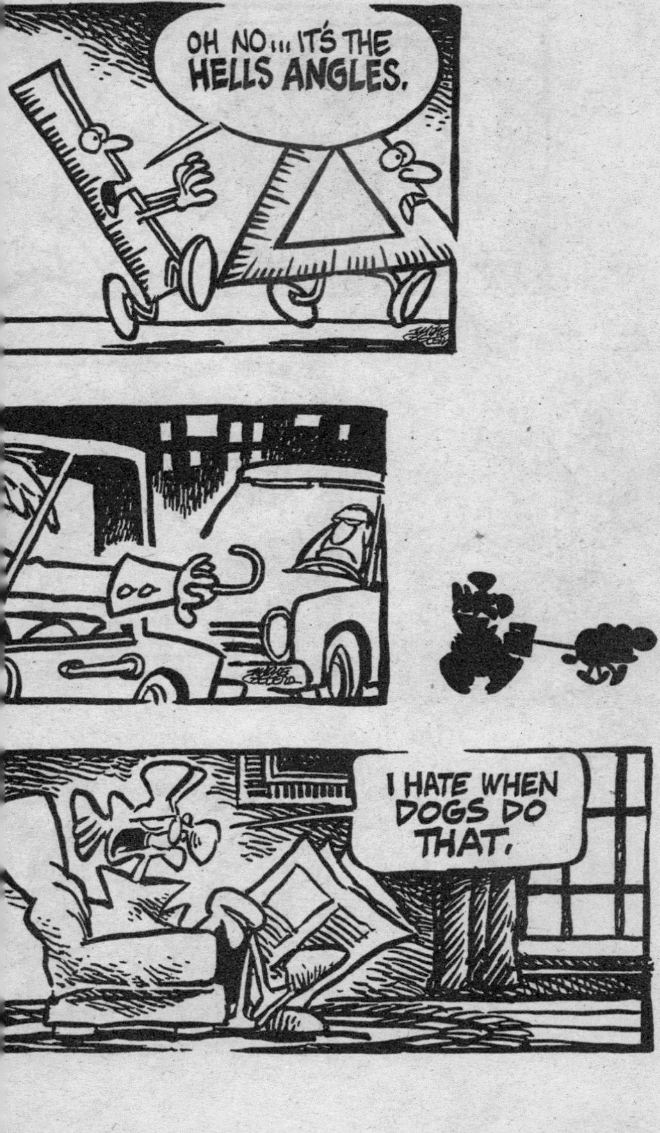
OH NO... IT'S THE HELLS ANGLES.
I HATE WHEN DOGS DO THAT.

BONK

HEY, GET AN AFTER LIFE...

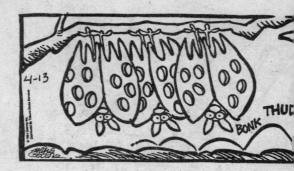

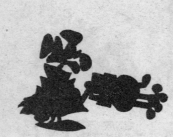

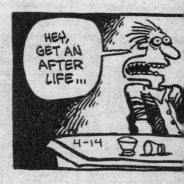

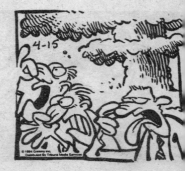

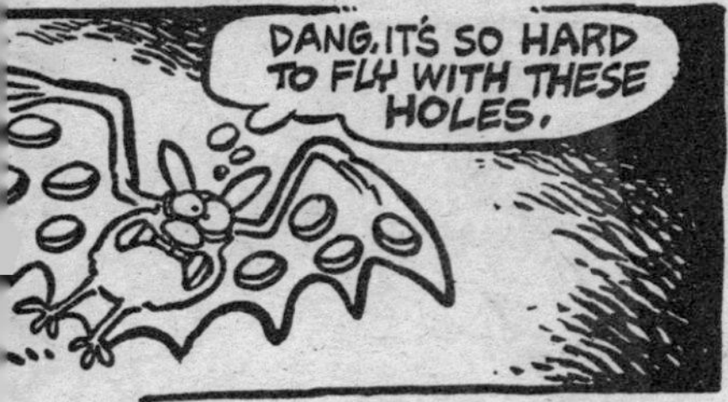
DANG, IT'S SO HARD TO FLY WITH THESE HOLES.

WHIFFLE BATS

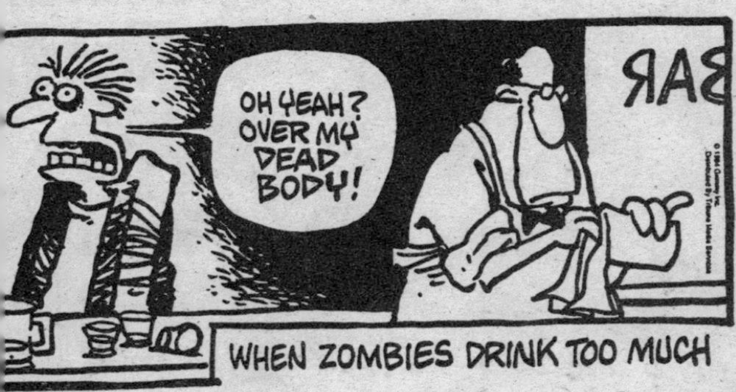
BAR
OH YEAH? OVER MY DEAD BODY!

WHEN ZOMBIES DRINK TOO MUCH

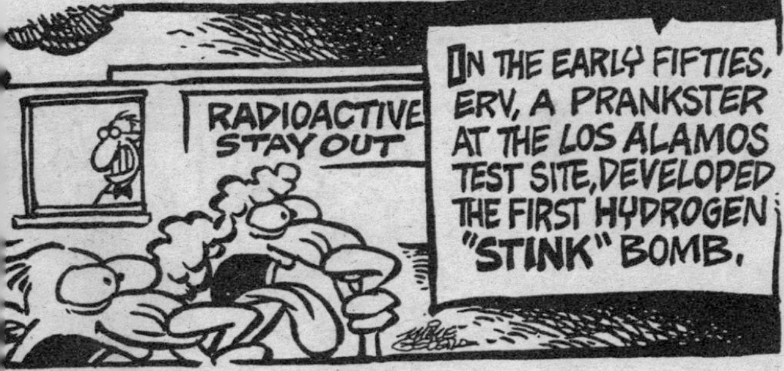
RADIOACTIVE STAY OUT
IN THE EARLY FIFTIES, ERV, A PRANKSTER AT THE LOS ALAMOS TEST SITE, DEVELOPED THE FIRST HYDROGEN "STINK" BOMB.

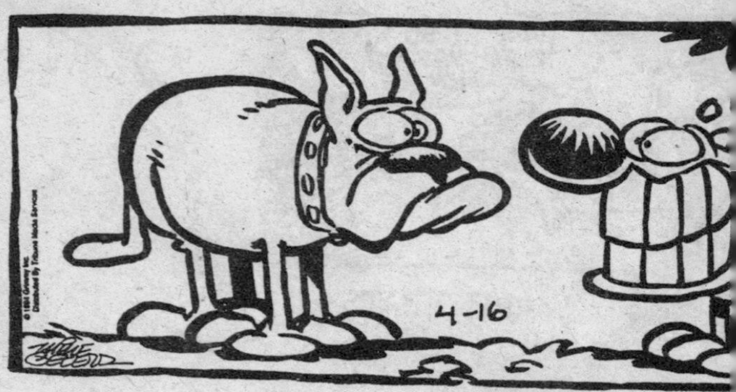
4-16

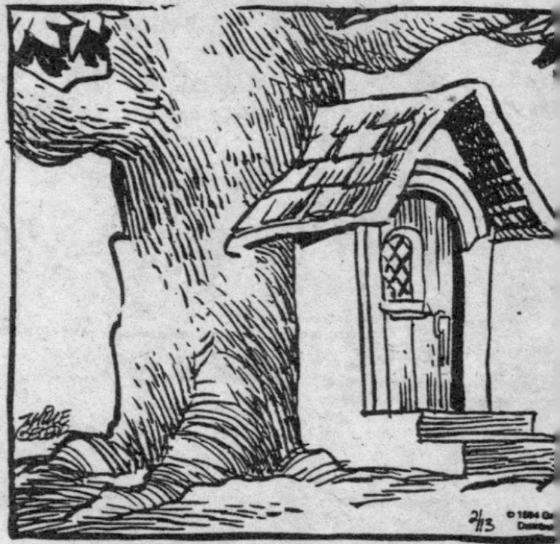
2/13

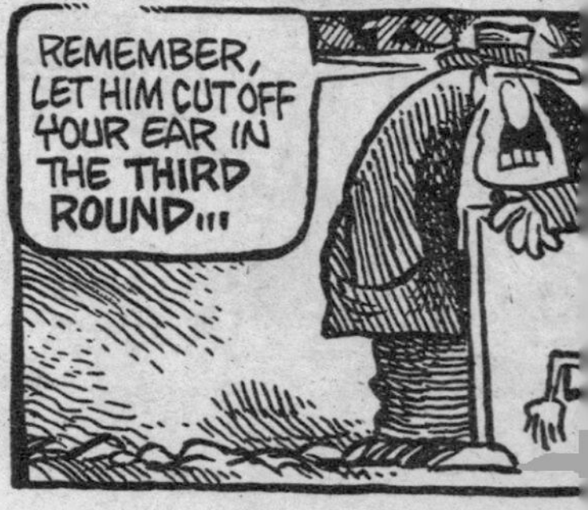
REMEMBER, LET HIM CUT OFF YOUR EAR IN THE THIRD ROUND...

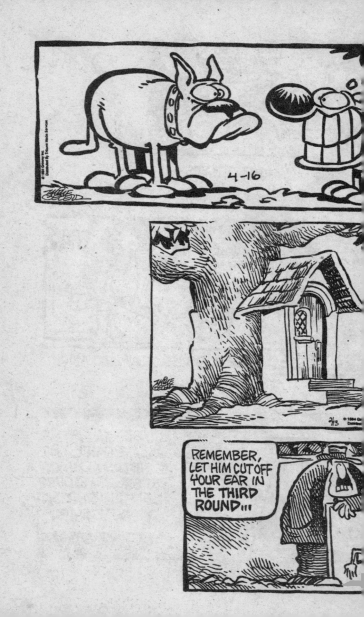

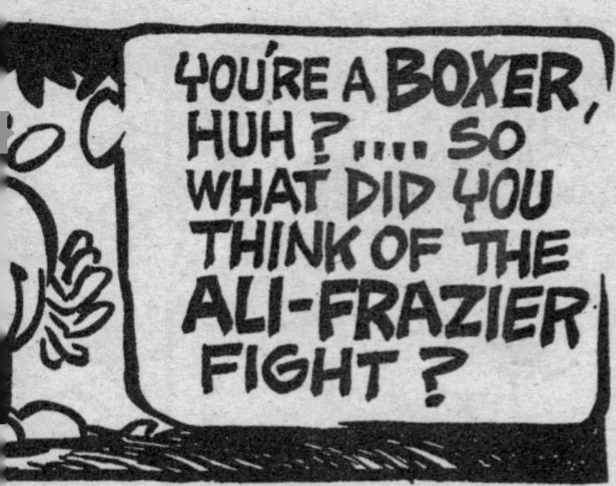
YOU'RE A BOXER, HUH ?.... SO WHAT DID YOU THINK OF THE ALI-FRAZIER FIGHT ?

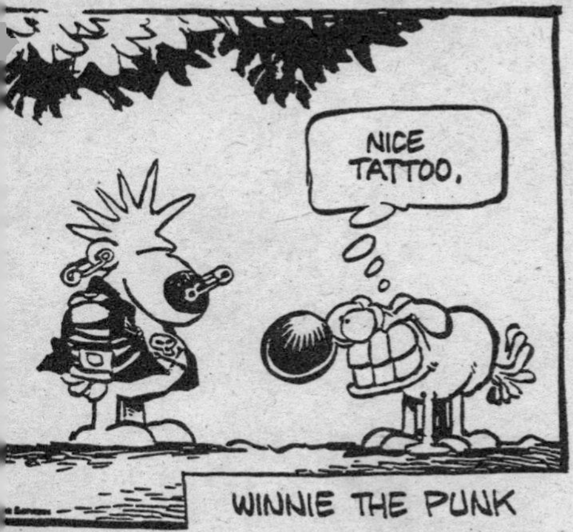
NICE TATTOO.

WINNIE THE PUNK

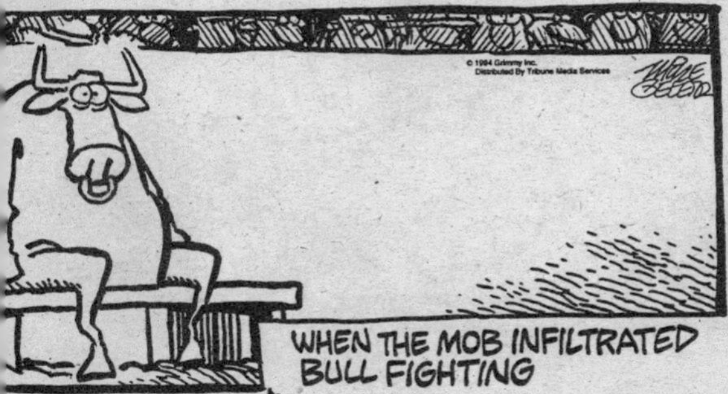
© 1994 Grimmy Inc.
Distributed By Tribune Media Services

WHEN THE MOB INFILTRATED BULL FIGHTING

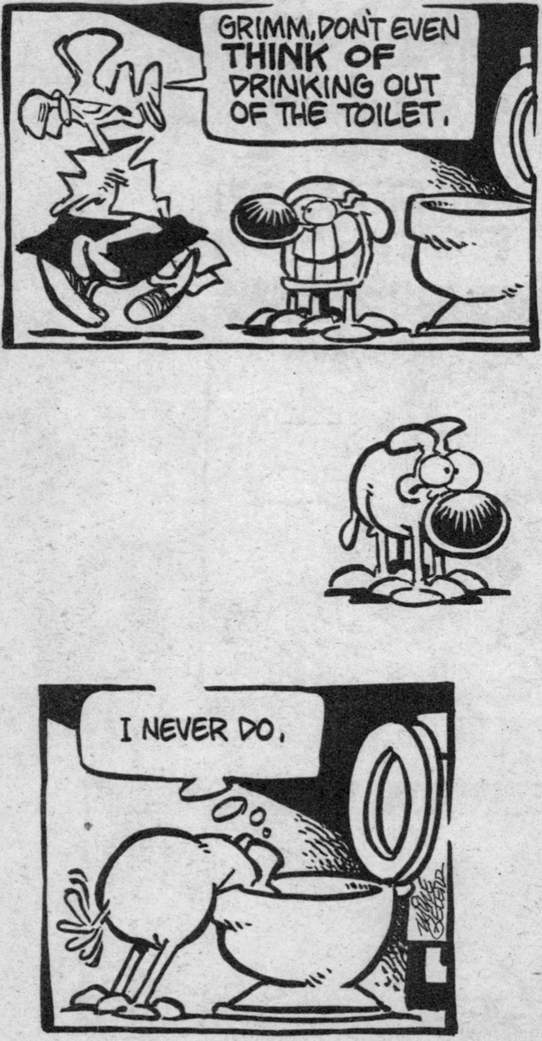
GRIMM, DON'T EVEN **THINK OF** DRINKING OUT OF THE TOILET.
I NEVER DO.

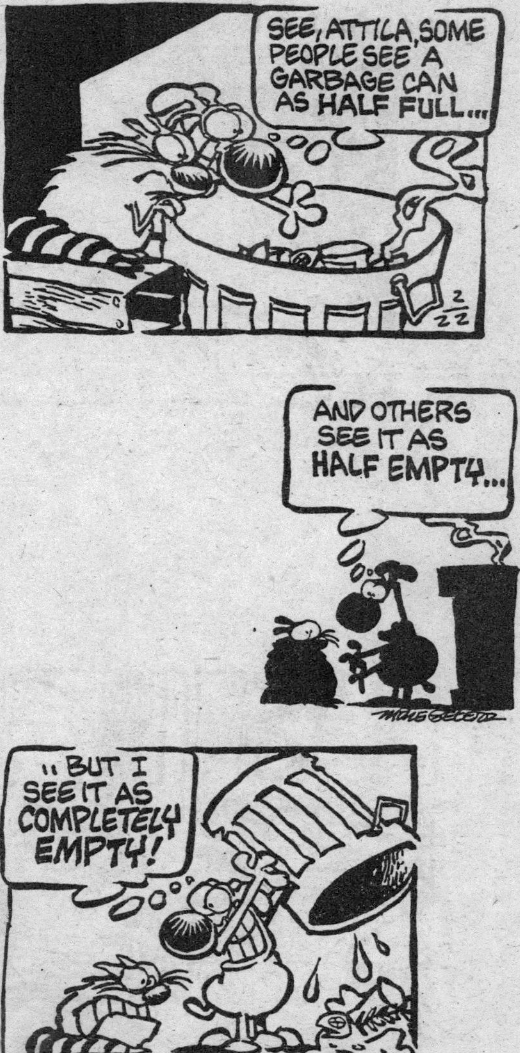
SEE, ATTICA, SOME PEOPLE SEE A GARBAGE CAN AS HALF FULL...
AND OTHERS SEE IT AS HALF EMPTY...
..BUT I SEE IT AS COMPLETELY EMPTY!

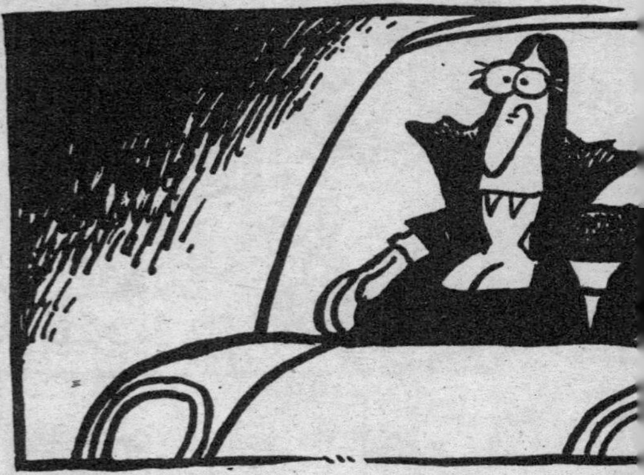

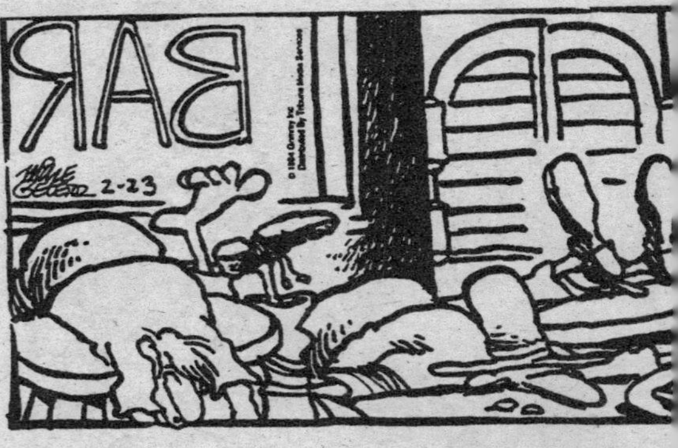
BAR
2-23
© 1994 Grimmy Inc
Distributed By Tribune Media Services

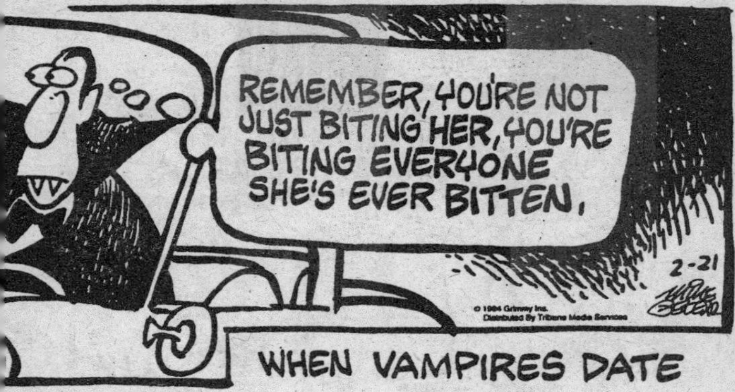
REMEMBER, YOU'RE NOT JUST BITING HER, YOU'RE BITING EVERYONE SHE'S EVER BITTEN.
2-21
© 1984 Grimmy Inc.
Distributed By Tribune Media Services

WHEN VAMPIRES DATE

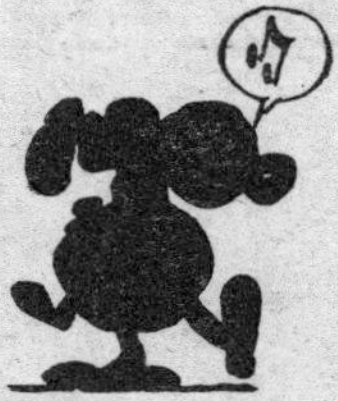

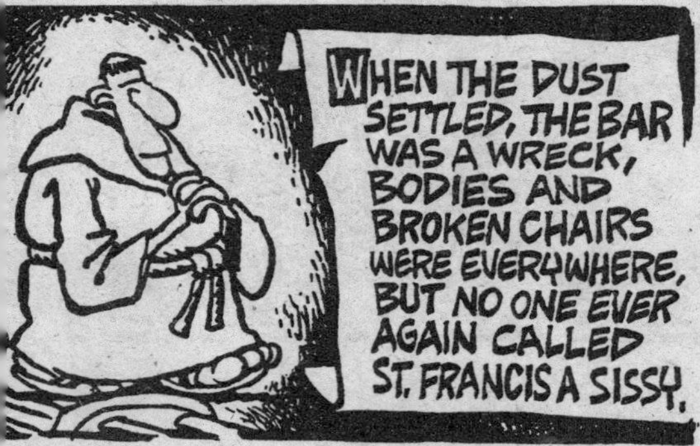
WHEN THE DUST SETTLED, THE BAR WAS A WRECK, BODIES AND BROKEN CHAIRS WERE EVERYWHERE, BUT NO ONE EVER AGAIN CALLED ST. FRANCIS A SISSY.

LOOK GRIMMY, MY SISTER'S CAT, SUMO, WILL BE STAYING WITH US FOR A WHILE.

QUICK, GET ME SIEGFRIED AND ROY!!

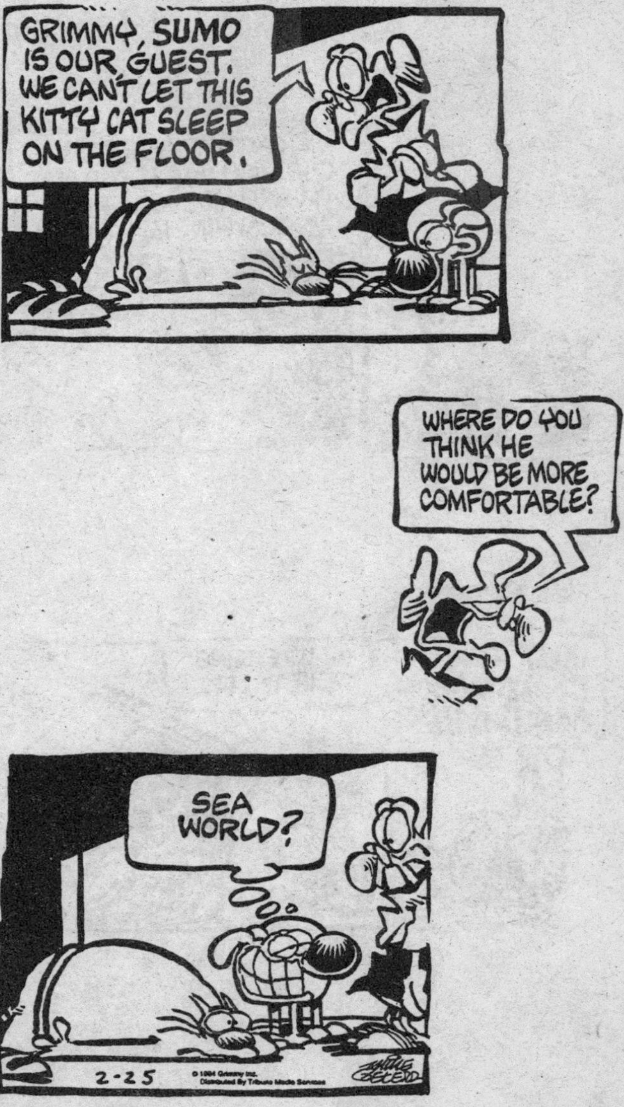

GRIMMY, SUMO IS OUR GUEST. WE CAN'T LET THIS KITTY CAT SLEEP ON THE FLOOR.
WHERE DO YOU THINK HE WOULD BE MORE COMFORTABLE?
SEA WORLD?
2-25

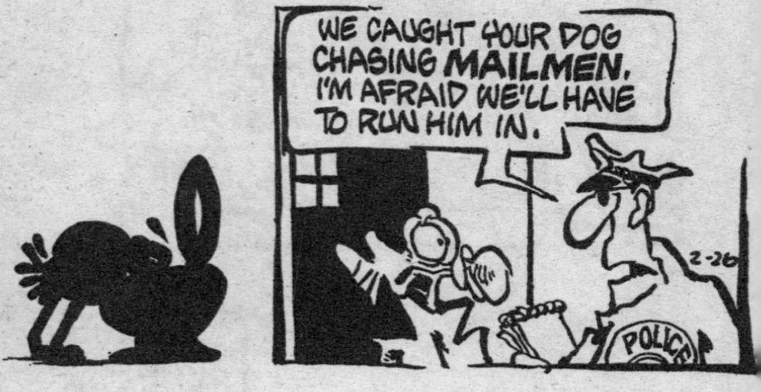
WE CAUGHT YOUR DOG CHASING MAILMEN. I'M AFRAID WE'LL HAVE TO RUN HIM IN.
POLICE
2-26

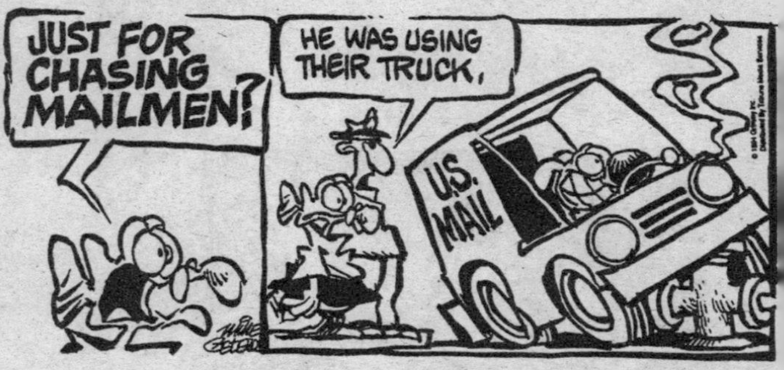
JUST FOR CHASING MAILMEN?
HE WAS USING THEIR TRUCK,
U.S. MAIL

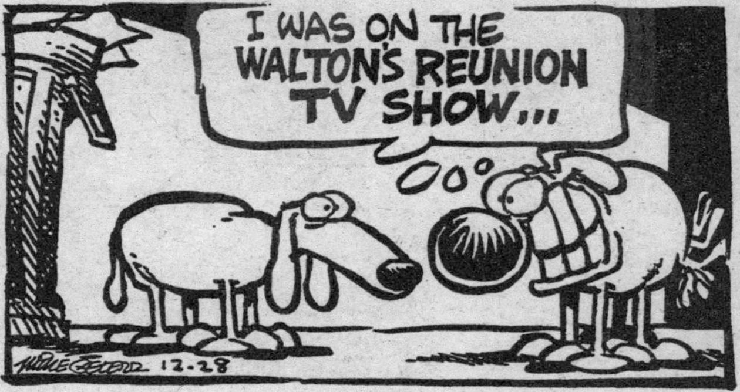
I WAS ON THE WALTON'S REUNION TV SHOW...
12-28

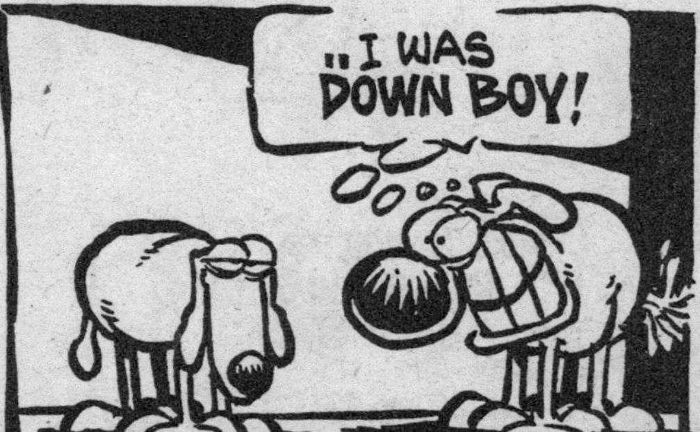
..I WAS DOWN BOY!

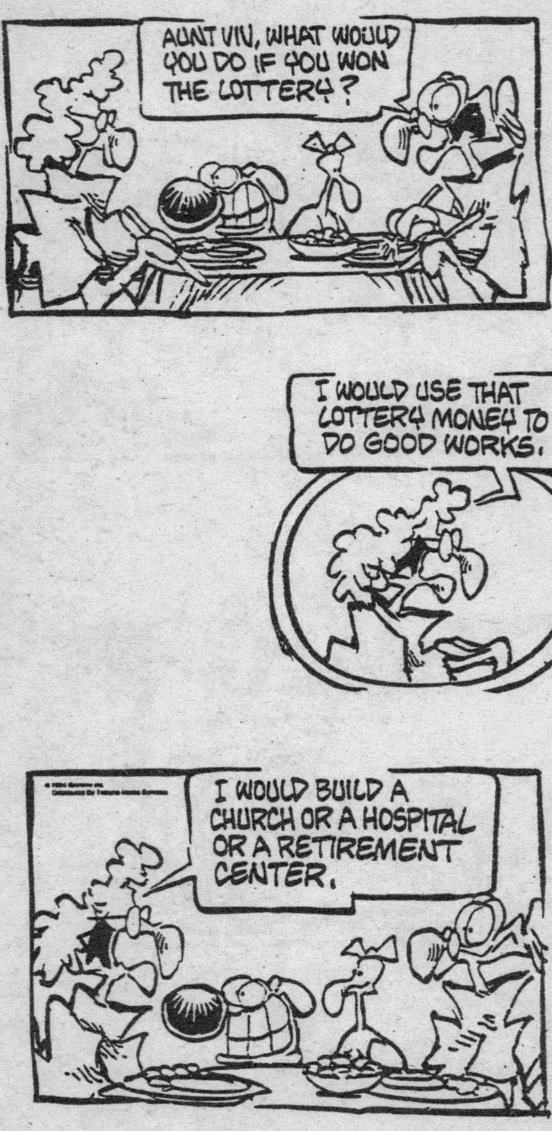
AUNT VIV, WHAT WOULD YOU DO IF YOU WON THE LOTTERY?
I WOULD USE THAT LOTTERY MONEY TO DO GOOD WORKS.
I WOULD BUILD A CHURCH OR A HOSPITAL OR A RETIREMENT CENTER.

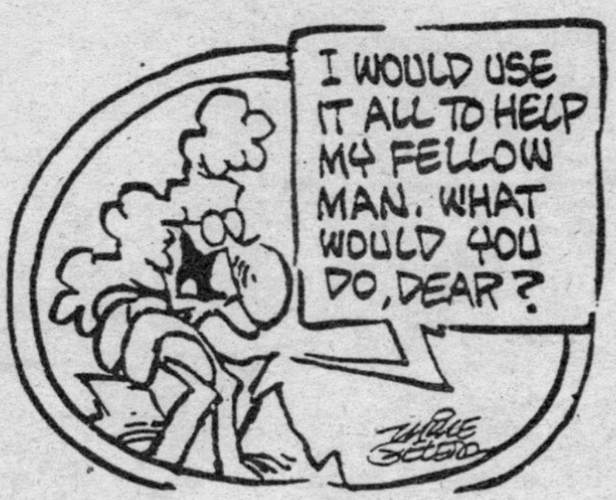
I WOULD USE IT ALL TO HELP MY FELLOW MAN. WHAT WOULD YOU DO, DEAR?

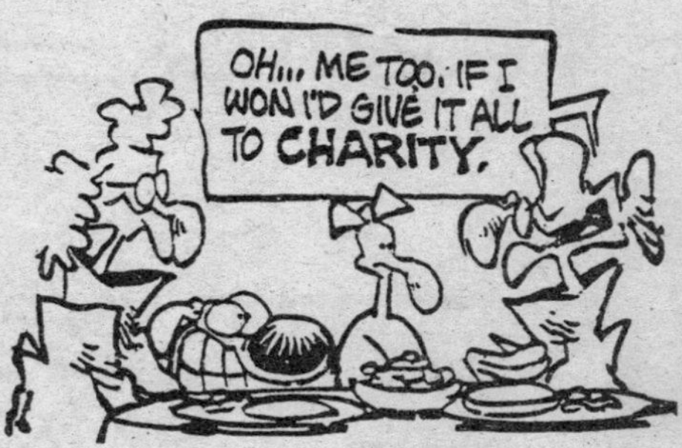
OH... ME TOO. IF I WON I'D GIVE IT ALL TO CHARITY.

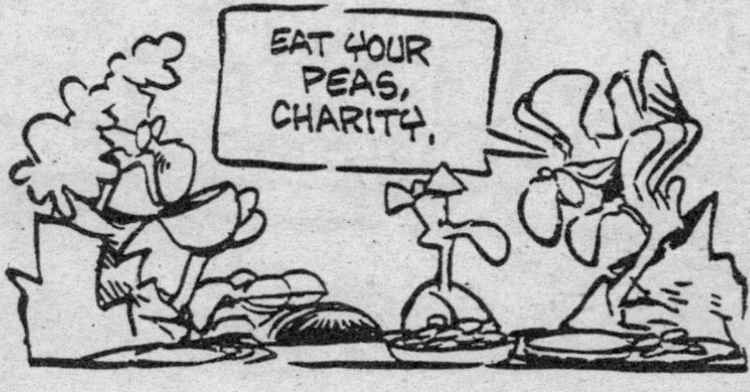
EAT YOUR PEAS, CHARITY.

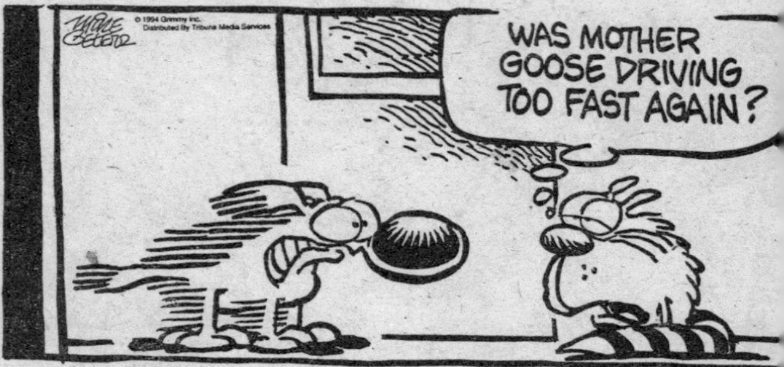
© 1994 Grimmy Inc.
Distributed By Tribune Media Services
WAS MOTHER GOOSE DRIVING TOO FAST AGAIN?

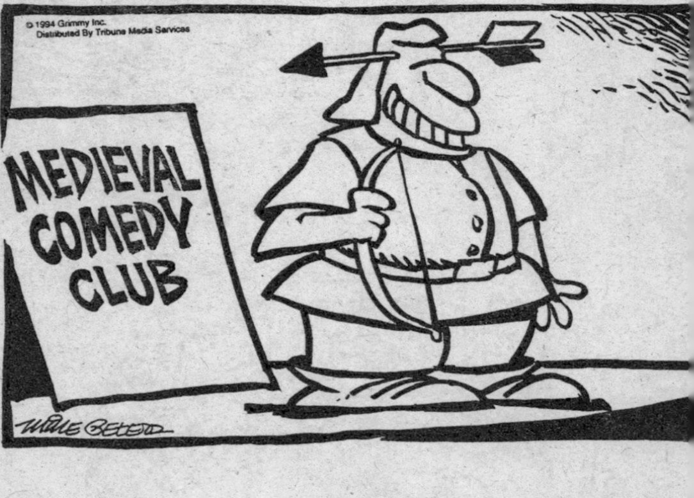
© 1994 Grimmy Inc.
Distributed By Tribune Media Services
MEDIEVAL COMEDY CLUB

WILLIAM TELL'S SON HAD A BUILT IN ADVANTAGE AT COMEDY CLUBS.

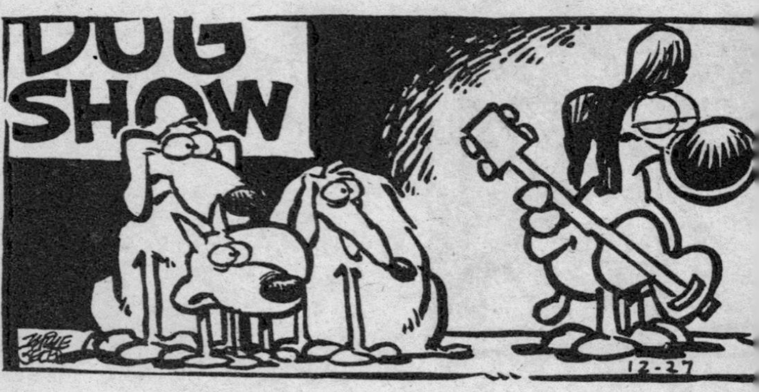
DOG
SHOW
12-27

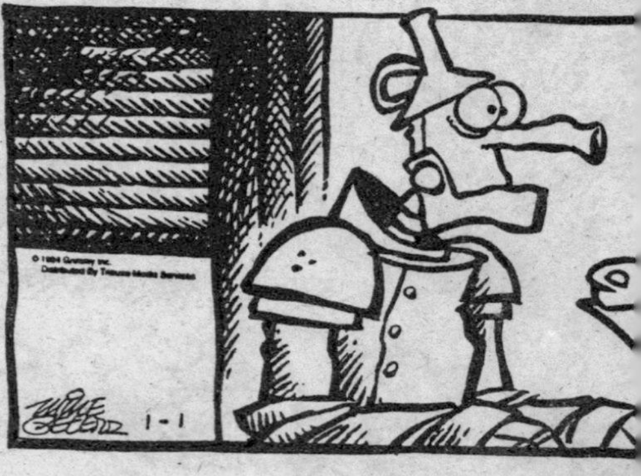
1-1

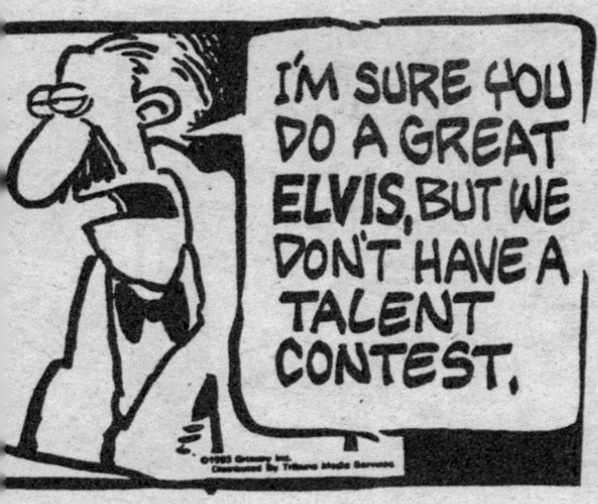
I'M SURE YOU DO A GREAT ELVIS, BUT WE DON'T HAVE A TALENT CONTEST.

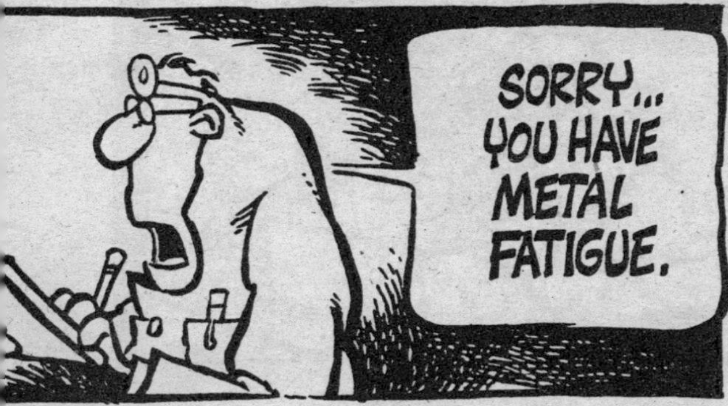
SORRY... YOU HAVE METAL FATIGUE.

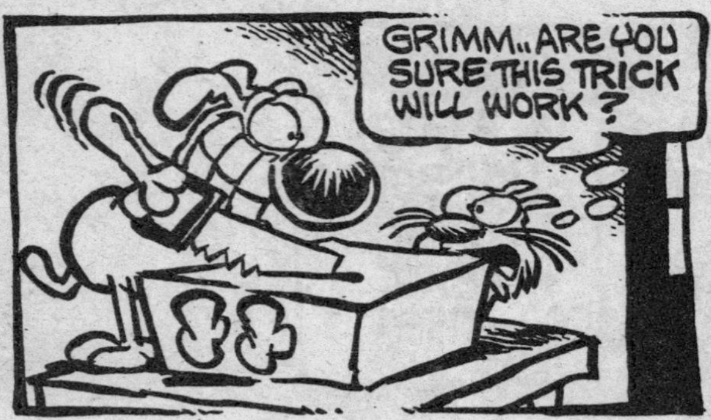
GRIMM.. ARE YOU SURE THIS TRICK WILL WORK?

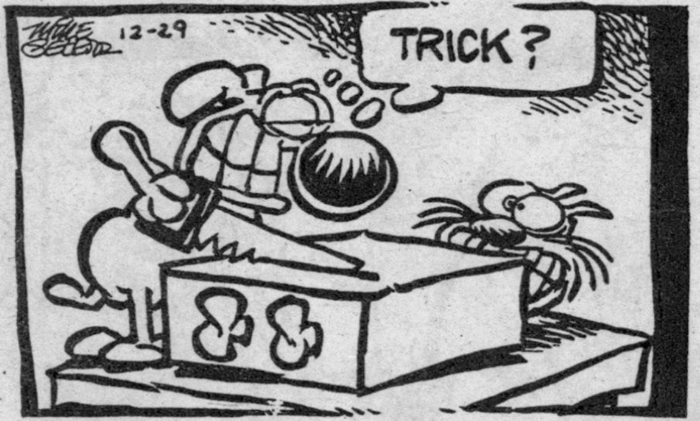
12-29
TRICK?

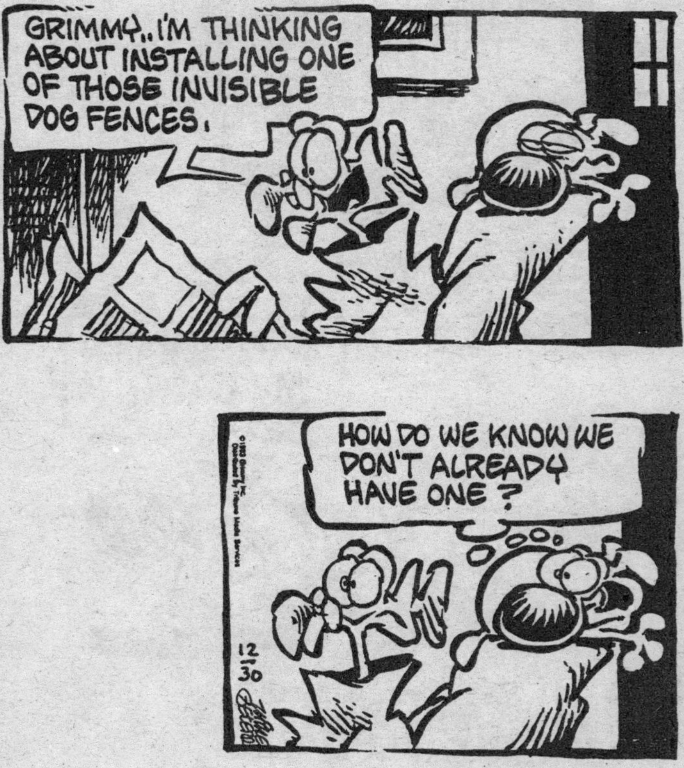
GRIMMY.. I'M THINKING ABOUT INSTALLING ONE OF THOSE INVISIBLE DOG FENCES.
HOW DO WE KNOW WE DON'T ALREADY HAVE ONE ?
Distributed by Tribune Media Services
12/30

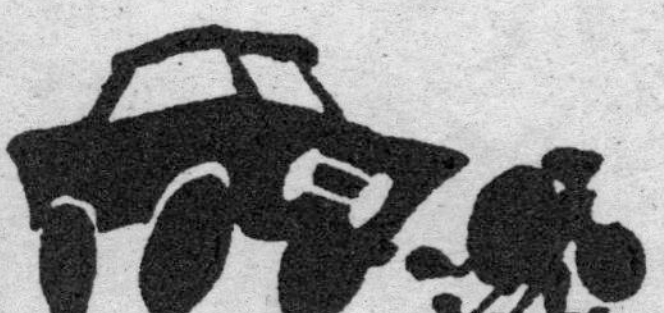

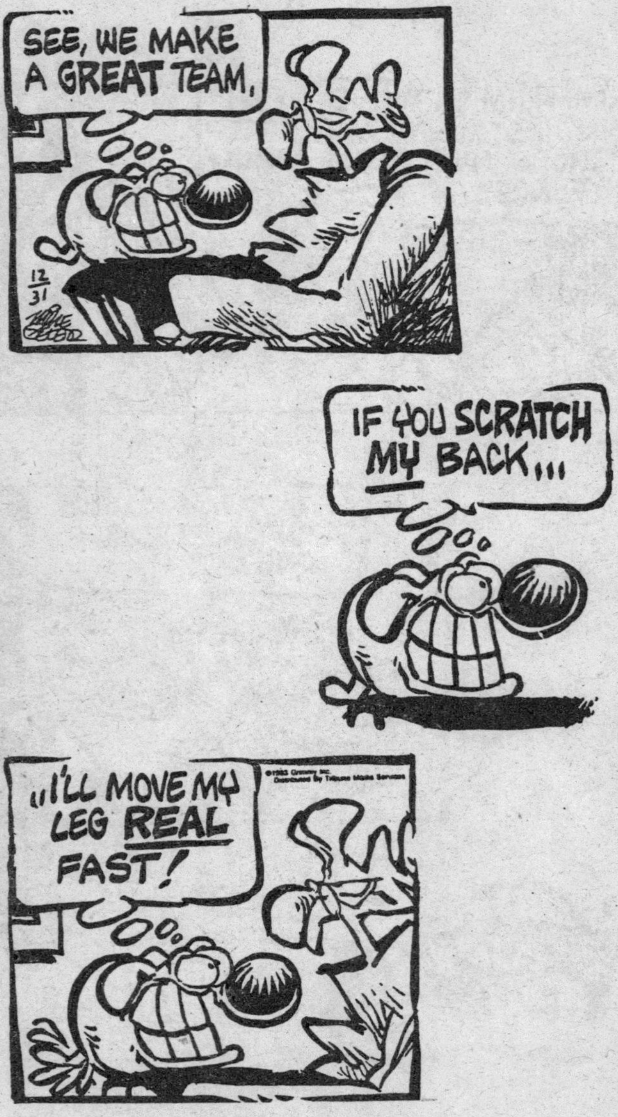
SEE, WE MAKE A GREAT TEAM,
12/31
IF YOU SCRATCH MY BACK...
...I'LL MOVE MY LEG REAL FAST!

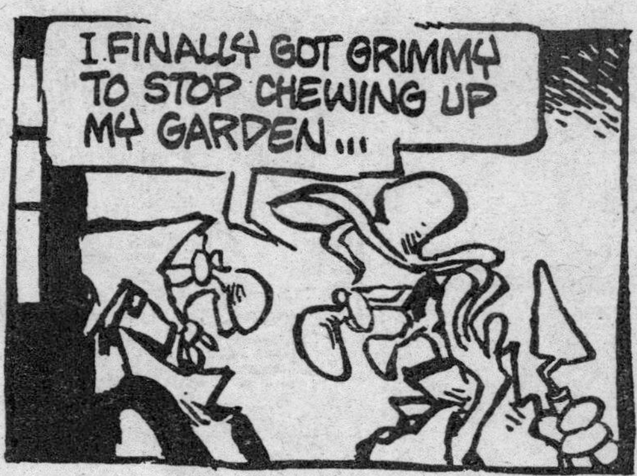
I FINALLY GOT GRIMMY TO STOP CHEWING UP MY GARDEN...

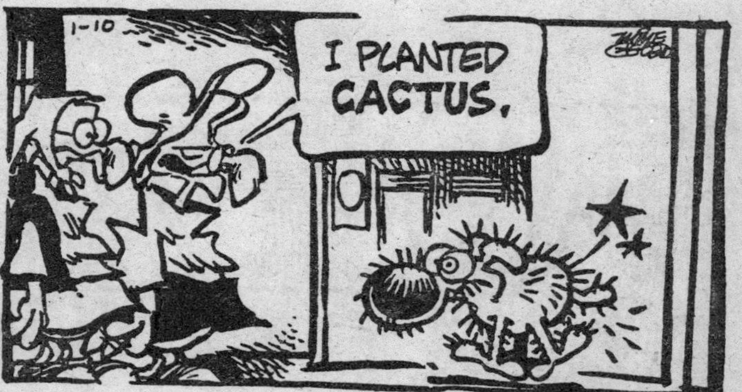
1-10
I PLANTED CACTUS.

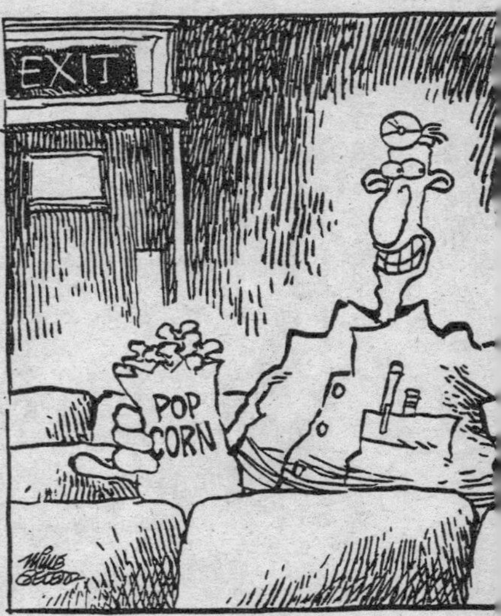
EXIT
POP CORN

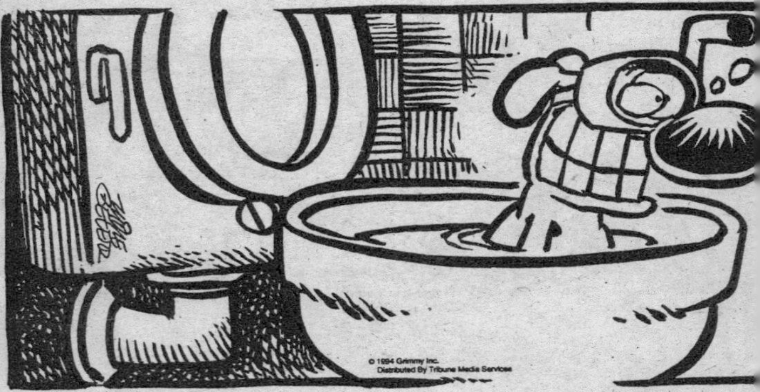
© 1994 Grimmy Inc.
Distributed By Tribune Media Services

YOUNG HEIMLICH'S <u>FIRST</u> MANEUVER

ATTILA, IT'S LIKE A TOTALLY OTHER WORLD DOWN THERE!

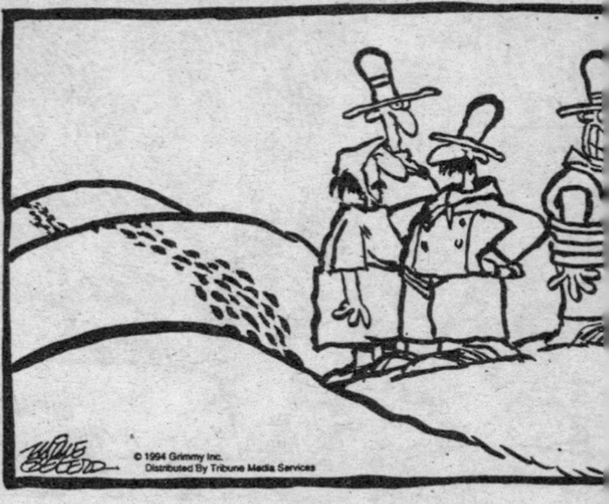
© 1994 Grimmy Inc.
Distributed By Tribune Media Services

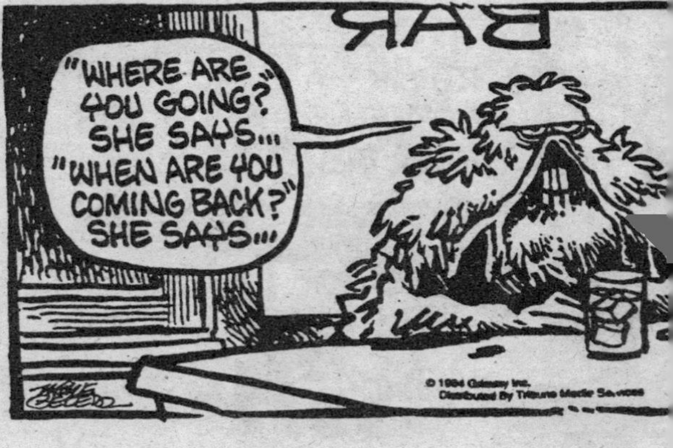
BAR
"WHERE ARE YOU GOING?" SHE SAYS... "WHEN ARE YOU COMING BACK?" SHE SAYS...
© 1994 Grimmy Inc.
Distributed By Tribune Media Services

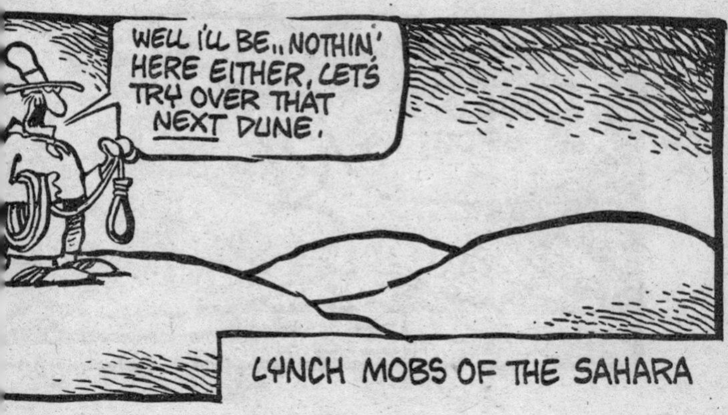
WELL I'LL BE.. NOTHIN' HERE EITHER, LET'S TRY OVER THAT NEXT DUNE.
LYNCH MOBS OF THE SAHARA

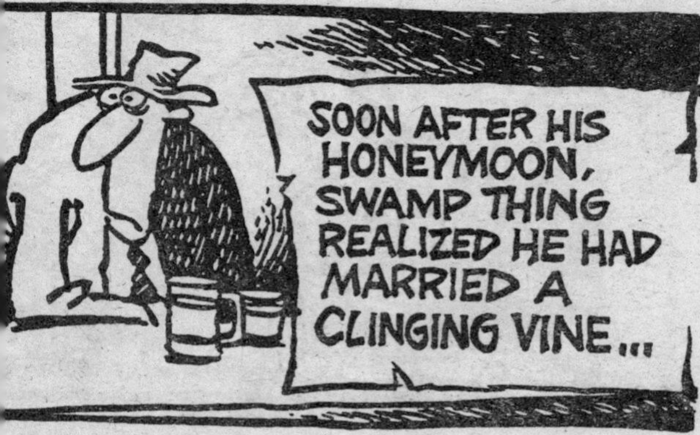
SOON AFTER HIS HONEYMOON, SWAMP THING REALIZED HE HAD MARRIED A CLINGING VINE...

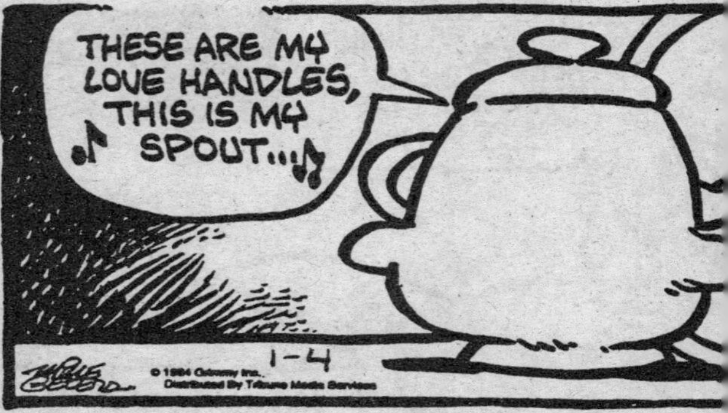
THESE ARE MY LOVE HANDLES, THIS IS MY SPOUT...
1-4
© 1994 Grimmy Inc.
Distributed By Tribune Media Services

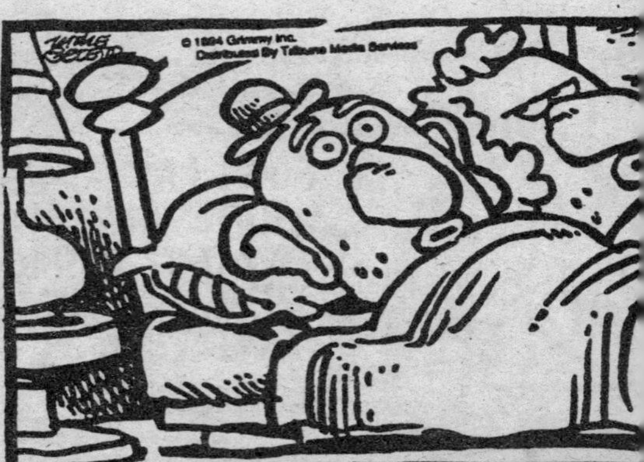
© 1994 Grimmy Inc.
Distributed By Tribune Media Services

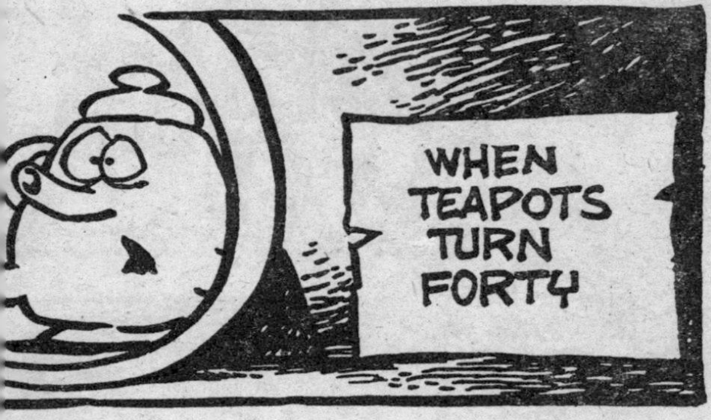
WHEN TEAPOTS TURN FORTY

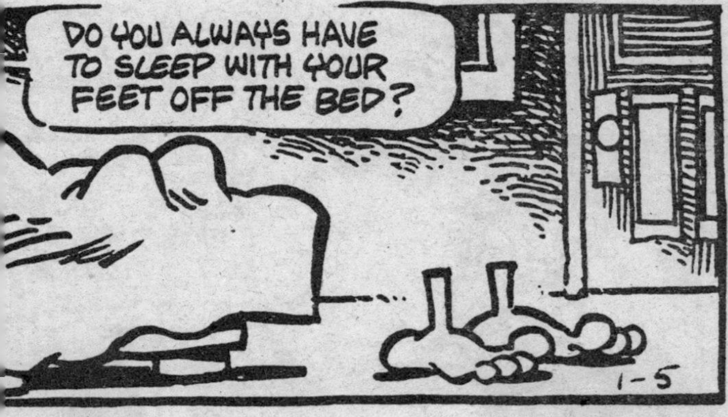
DO YOU ALWAYS HAVE TO SLEEP WITH YOUR FEET OFF THE BED?
1-5

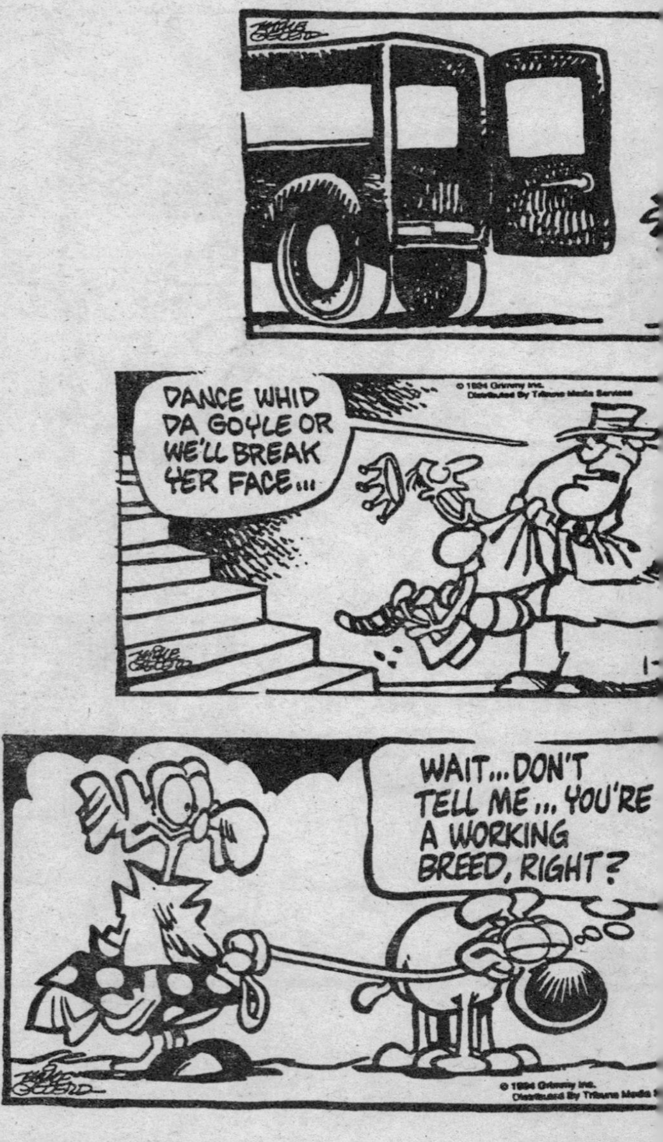
© 1994 Grimmy Inc.
Distributed By Tribune Media Services
DANCE WHID DA GOYLE OR WE'LL BREAK YER FACE...
WAIT... DON'T TELL ME... YOU'RE A WORKING BREED, RIGHT?
© 1994 Grimmy Inc.

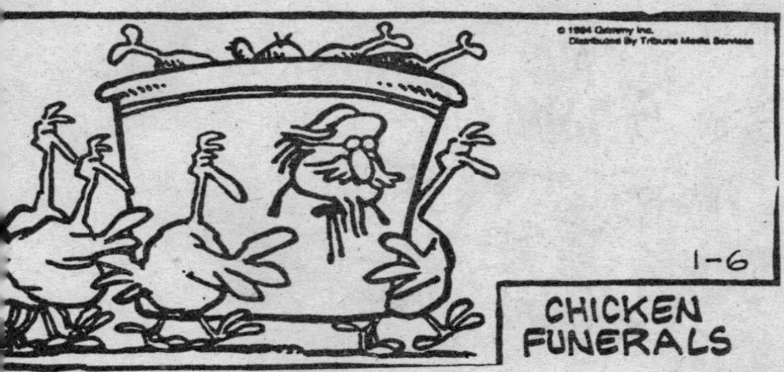

1-6
CHICKEN FUNERALS


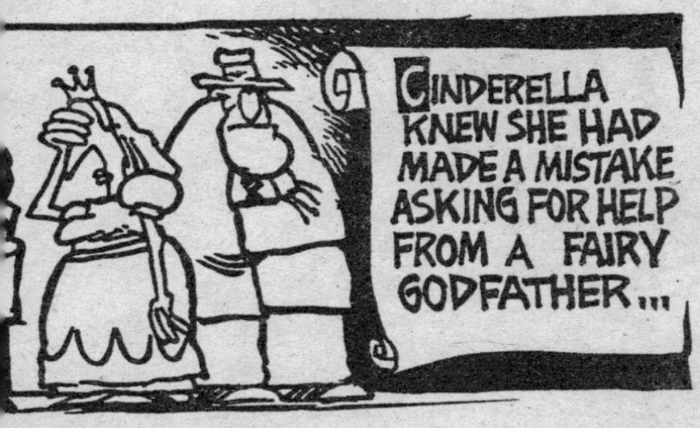

CINDERELLA KNEW SHE HAD MADE A MISTAKE ASKING FOR HELP FROM A FAIRY GODFATHER...


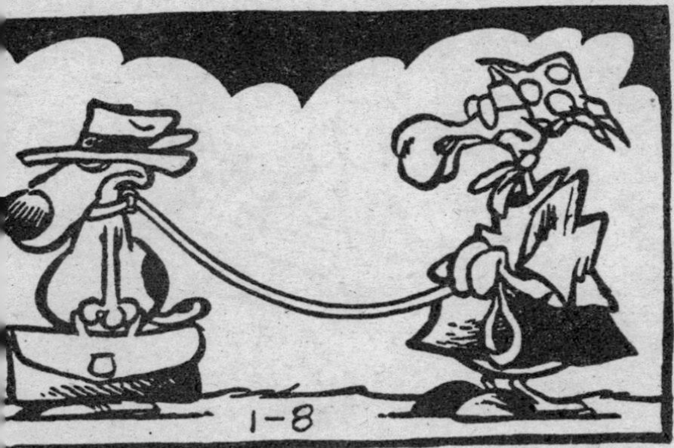

1-8

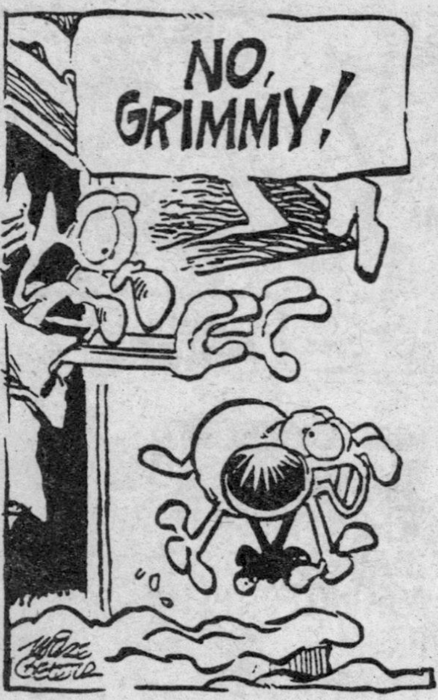
NO, GRIMMY!

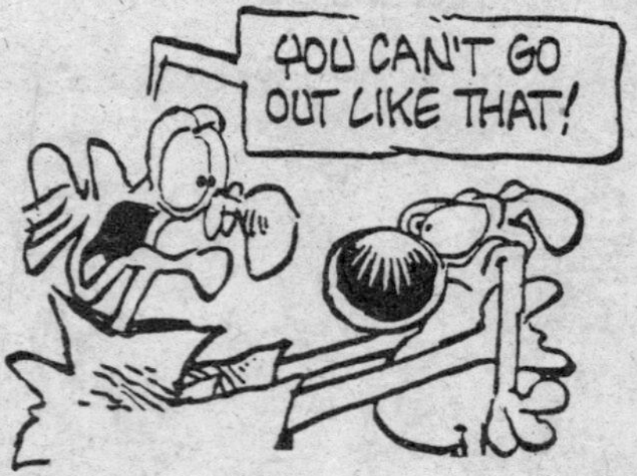
YOU CAN'T GO OUT LIKE THAT!

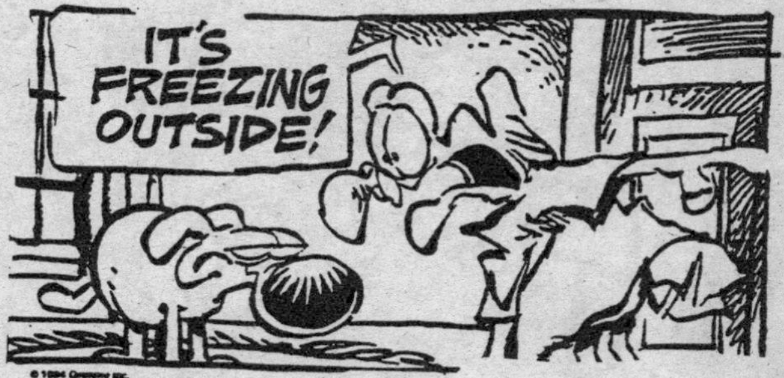
IT'S FREEZING OUTSIDE!

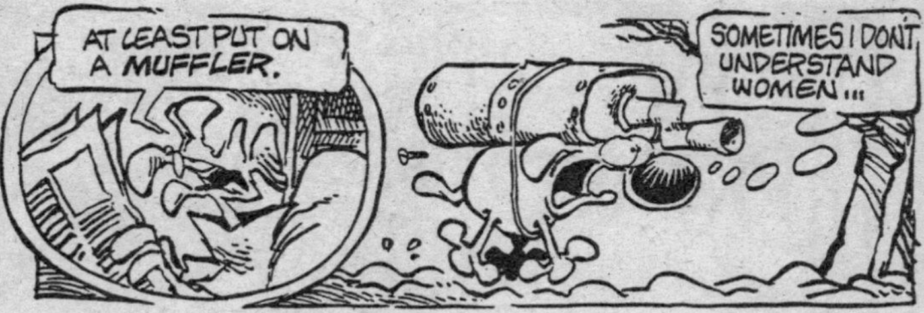
AT LEAST PUT ON A MUFFLER.
SOMETIMES I DON'T UNDERSTAND WOMEN...

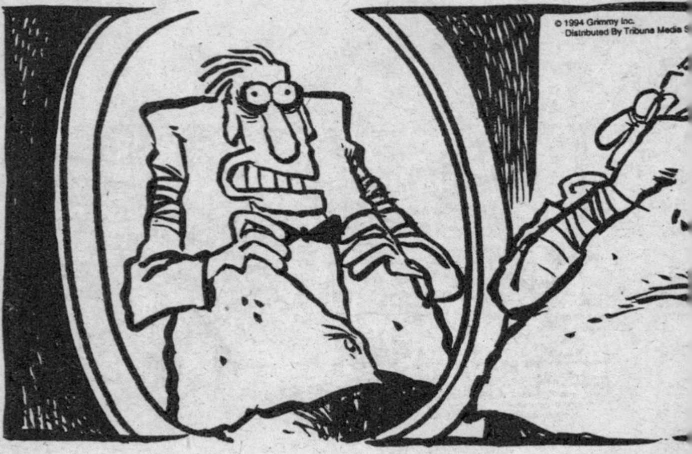
© 1994 Grimmy Inc.
Distributed By Tribune Media

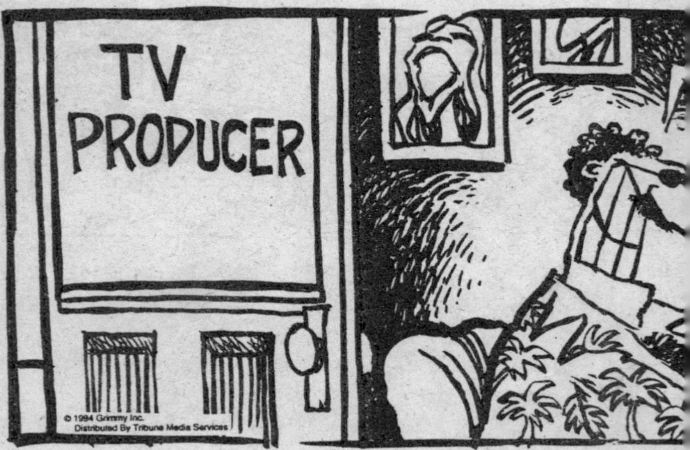
TV
PRODUCER
© 1994 Grimmy Inc.
Distributed By Tribune Media Services

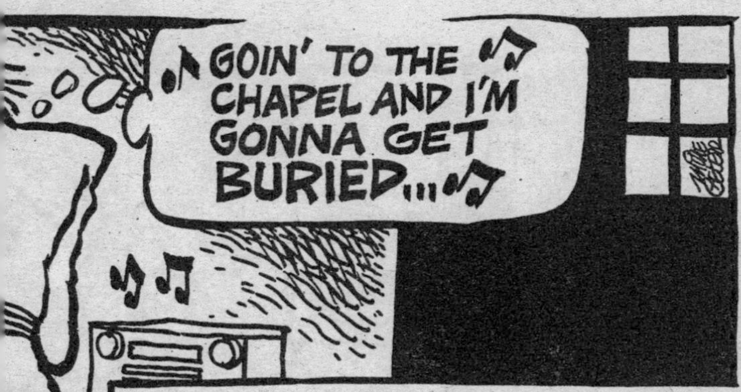
GOIN' TO THE CHAPEL AND I'M GONNA GET BURIED...

ZOMBIE GOLDEN OLDIES

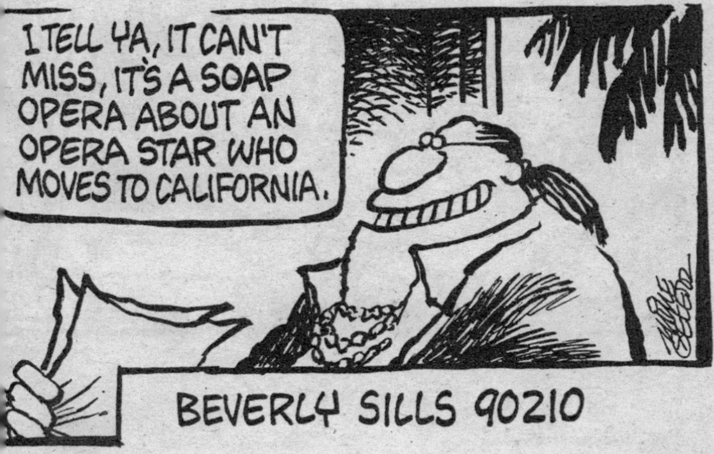
I TELL YA, IT CAN'T MISS, IT'S A SOAP OPERA ABOUT AN OPERA STAR WHO MOVES TO CALIFORNIA.

BEVERLY SILLS 90210

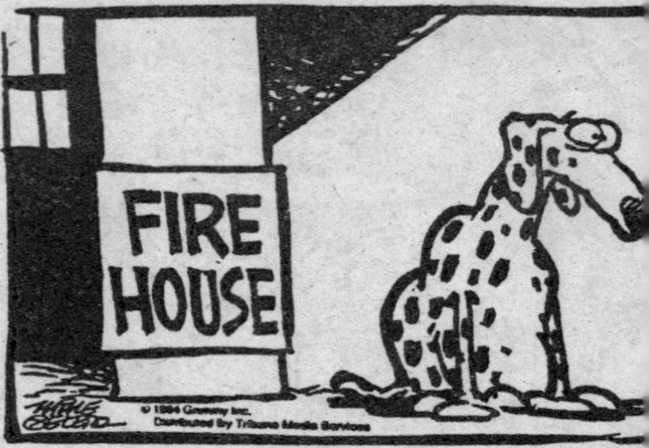
FIRE
HOUSE

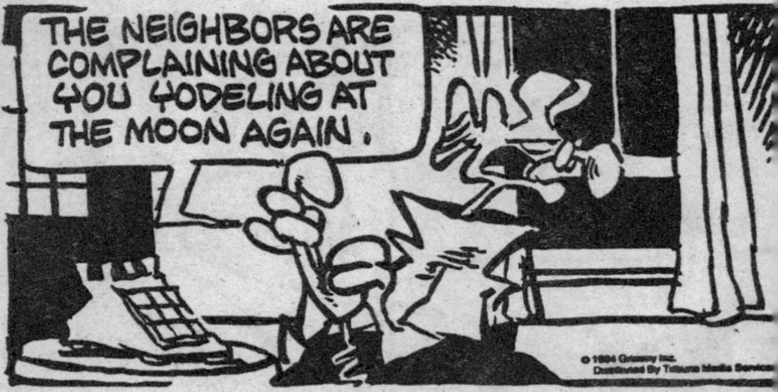
THE NEIGHBORS ARE COMPLAINING ABOUT YOU YODELING AT THE MOON AGAIN.

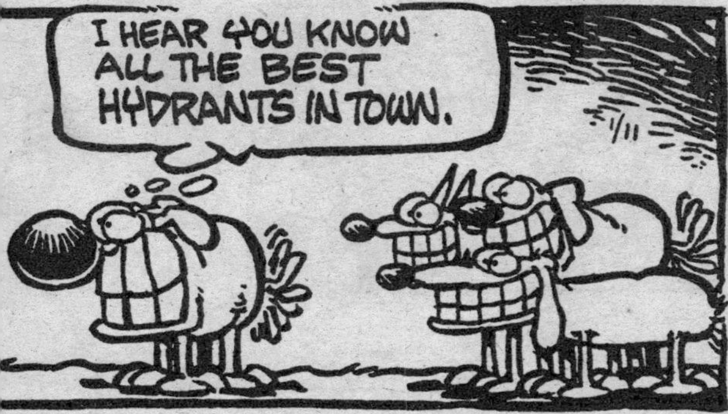
I HEAR YOU KNOW ALL THE BEST HYDRANTS IN TOWN.

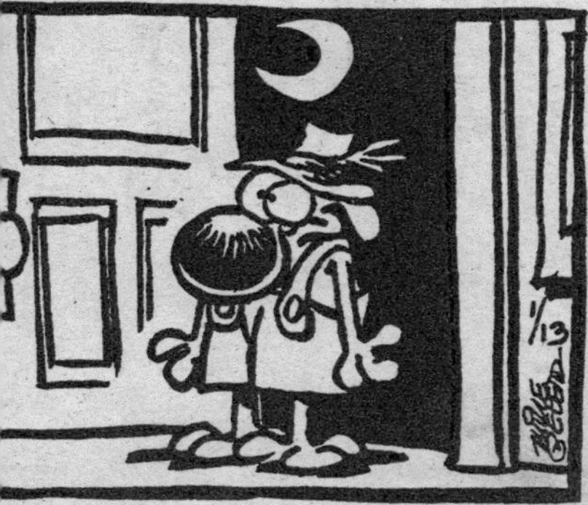

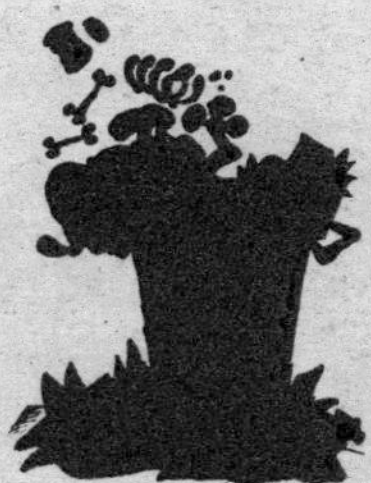

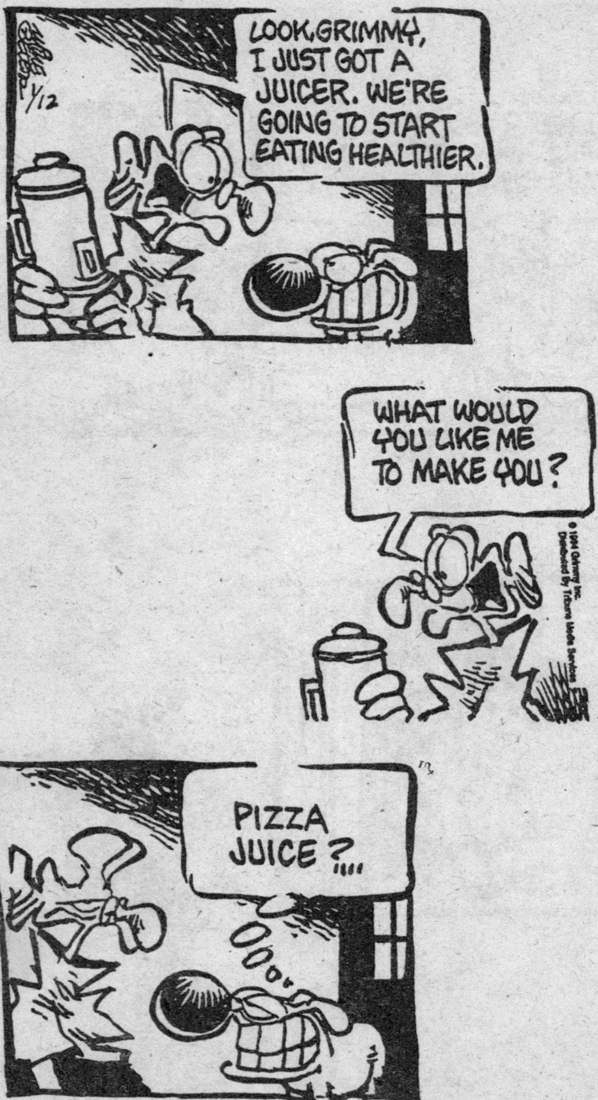
1/12
LOOK, GRIMMY, I JUST GOT A JUICER. WE'RE GOING TO START EATING HEALTHIER.
WHAT WOULD YOU LIKE ME TO MAKE YOU?
© 1994 Grimmy Inc.
Distributed by Tribune Media Services
PIZZA JUICE?....
OOOo.

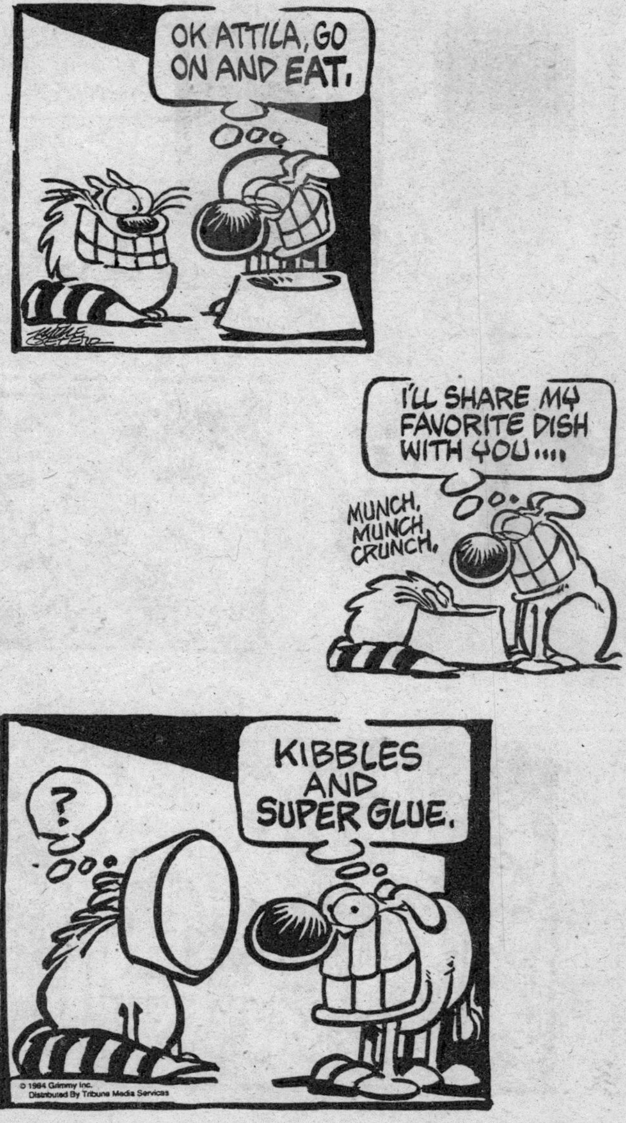
OK ATTILA, GO ON AND EAT.
I'LL SHARE MY FAVORITE DISH WITH YOU.....
MUNCH. MUNCH CRUNCH.
?
KIBBLES AND SUPER GLUE.
© 1984 Grimmy Inc.
Distributed By Tribune Media Services

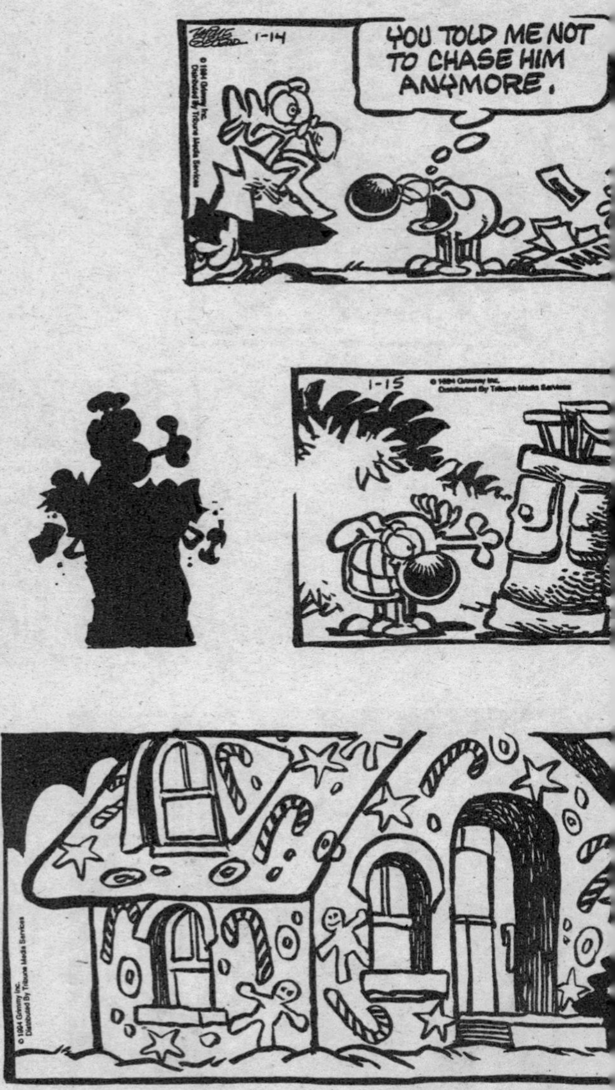
1-14
© 1984 Grimmy Inc.
Distributed By Tribune Media Services
YOU TOLD ME NOT TO CHASE HIM ANYMORE.
1-15
© 1984 Grimmy Inc.
Distributed By Tribune Media Services
© 1984 Grimmy Inc.
Distributed By Tribune Media Services

PSST.. WATCH OUT FOR THE **DOG LEG** ON THE LEFT.

YEP, WE HAVE TO FUMIGATE, LOOKS LIKE YOU'VE GOT A NEST OF CHILDREN.

PEST CONTROL

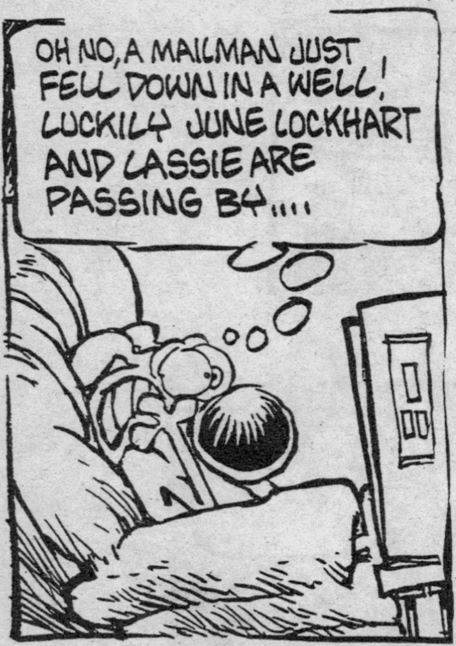
OH NO, A MAILMAN JUST FELL DOWN IN A WELL! LUCKILY JUNE LOCKHART AND LASSIE ARE PASSING BY....

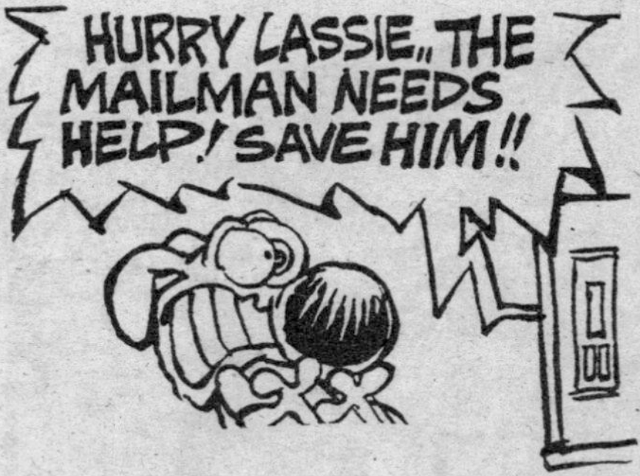
HURRY LASSIE.. THE MAILMAN NEEDS HELP! SAVE HIM!!

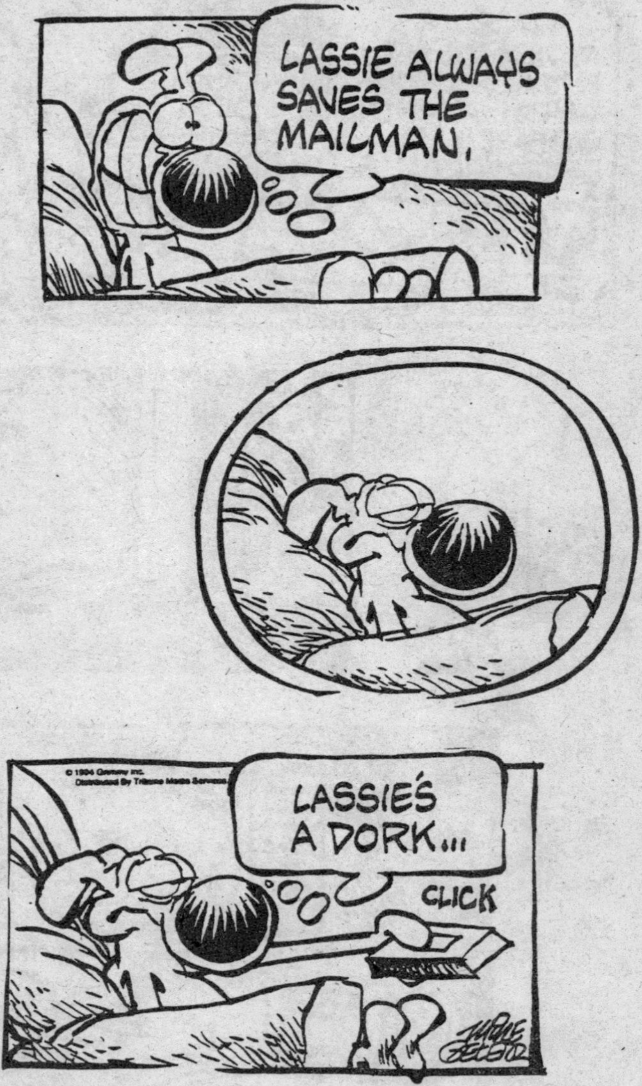
LASSIE ALWAYS SAVES THE MAILMAN.
LASSIE'S A DORK...
CLICK

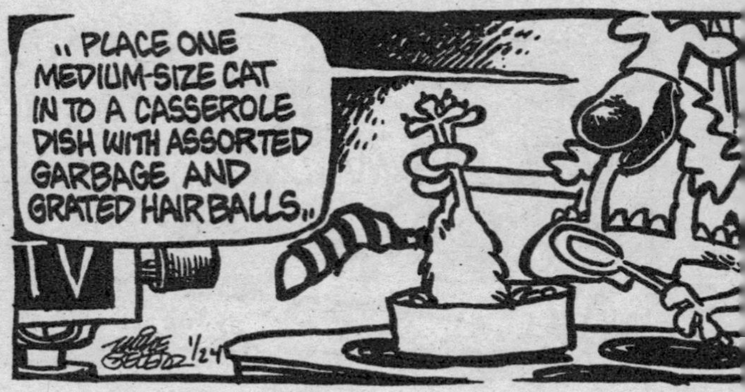
.. PLACE ONE MEDIUM-SIZE CAT IN TO A CASSEROLE DISH WITH ASSORTED GARBAGE AND GRATED HAIR BALLS..
TV
1/24

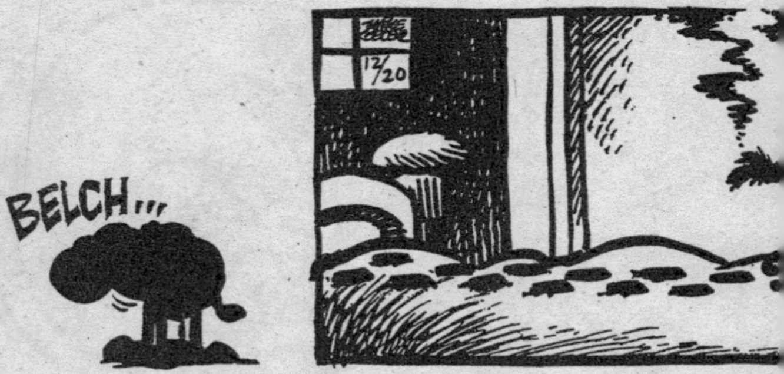
12/20
BELCH...

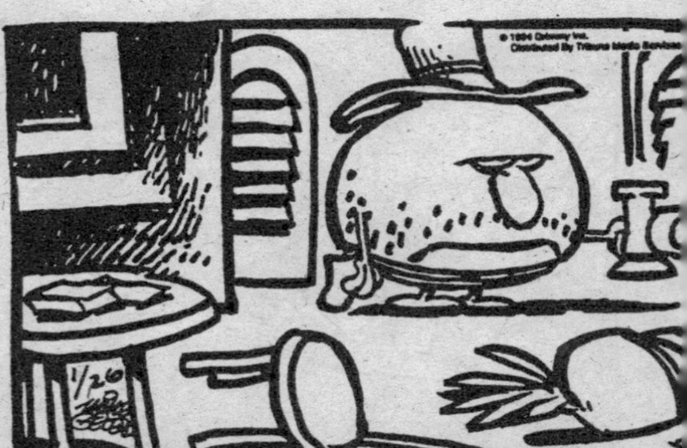
1/26

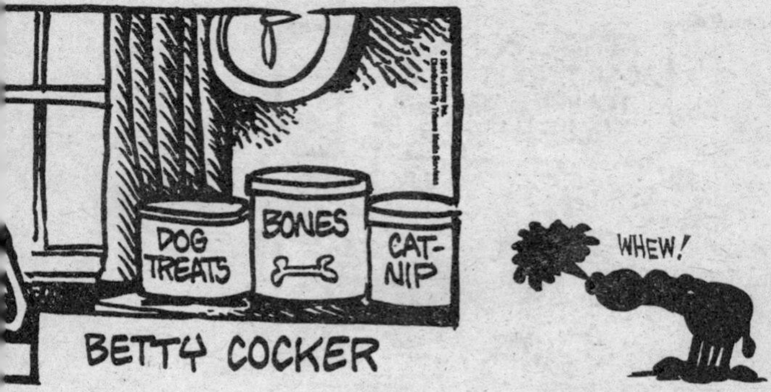
DOG TREATS
BONES
CAT-NIP
BETTY COCKER
WHEW!

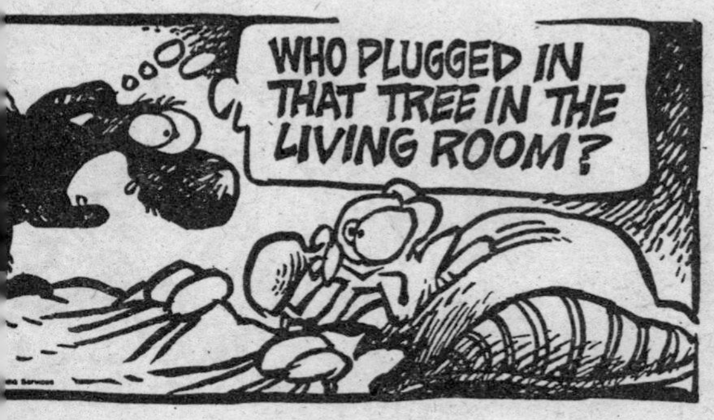
WHO PLUGGED IN THAT TREE IN THE LIVING ROOM?

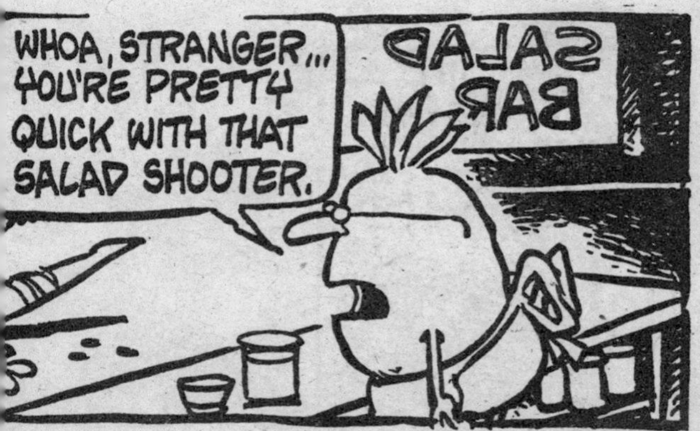
WHOA, STRANGER... YOU'RE PRETTY QUICK WITH THAT SALAD SHOOTER.
SALAD BAR

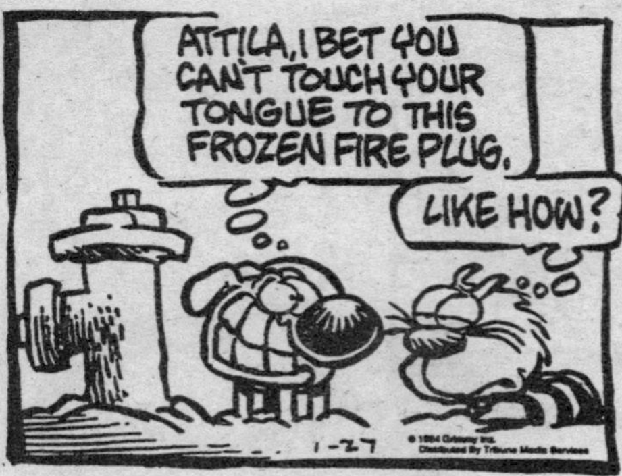
ATTILA, I BET YOU CAN'T TOUCH YOUR TONGUE TO THIS FROZEN FIRE PLUG.
LIKE HOW?
1-27
Distributed By Tribune Media Services

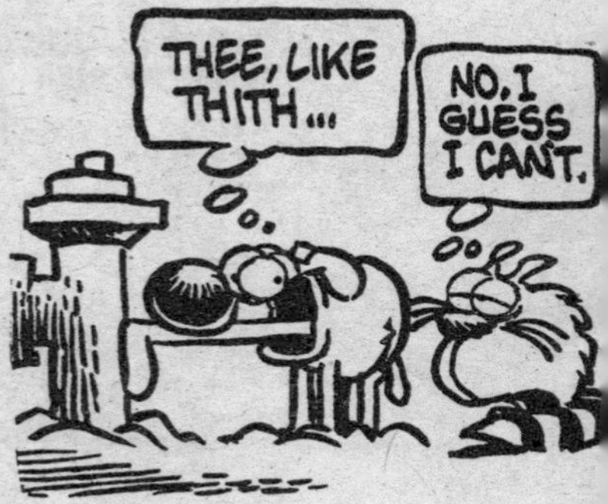
THEE, LIKE THITH...
NO, I GUESS I CAN'T.

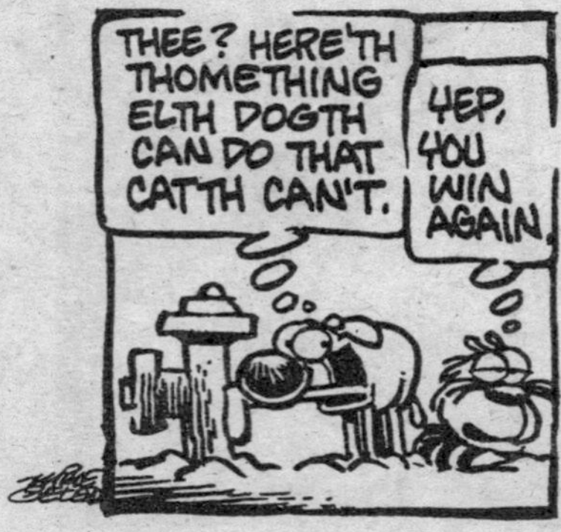
THEE? HERE'TH THOMETHING ELTH DOGTH CAN DO THAT CATTH CAN'T.
YEP, YOU WIN AGAIN.

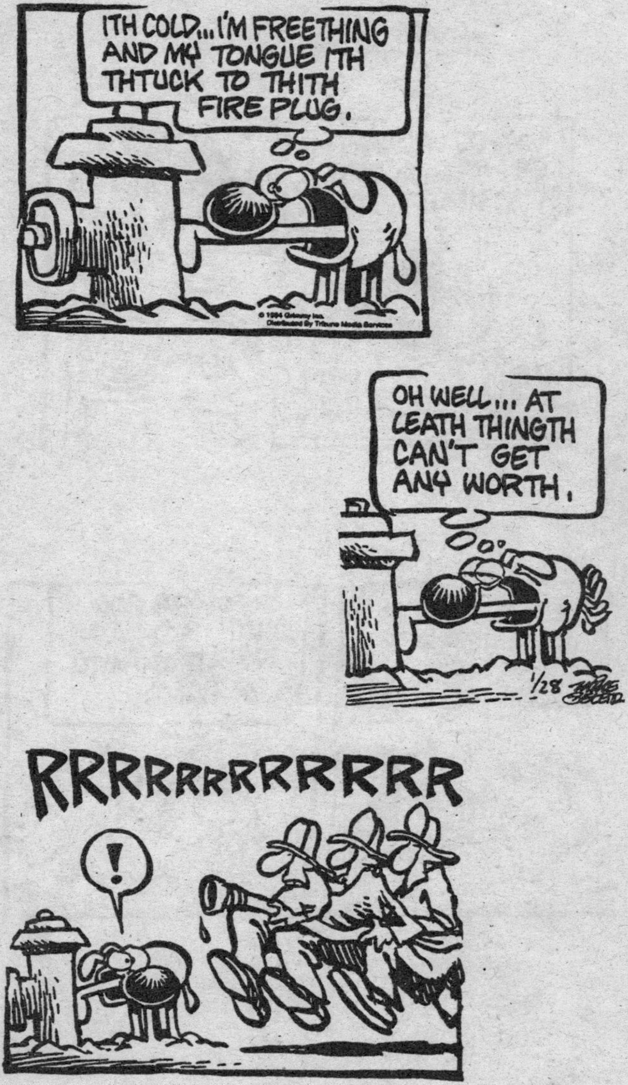
ITH COLD... I'M FREETHING AND MY TONGUE ITH THTUCK TO THITH FIRE PLUG.
© 1994 Grimmy Inc.
Distributed By Tribune Media Services
OH WELL... AT LEATH THINGTH CAN'T GET ANY WORTH.
1/28
RRRRRRRRRRRRR
!

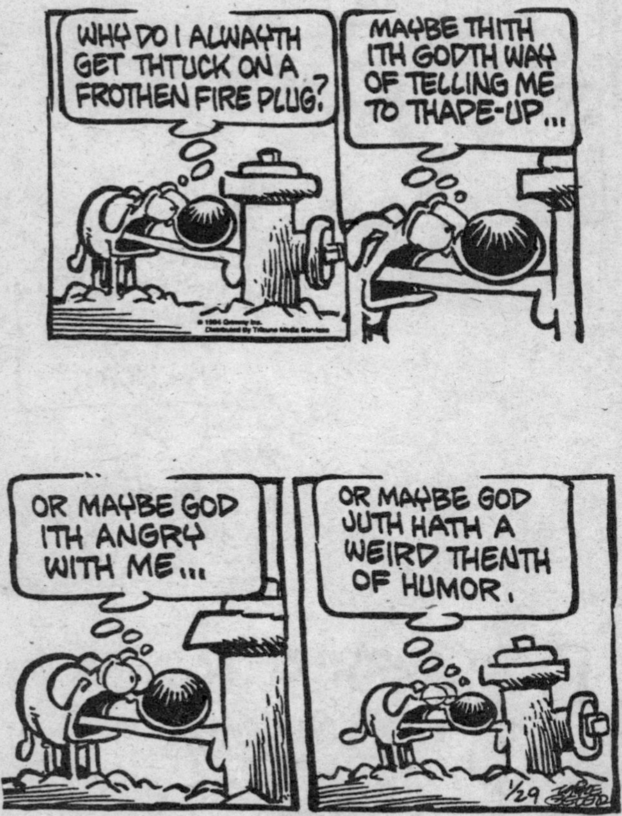
WHY DO I ALWAYTH GET THTUCK ON A FROTHEN FIRE PLUG?
MAYBE THITH ITH GODTH WAY OF TELLING ME TO THAPE-UP...
OR MAYBE GOD ITH ANGRY WITH ME...
OR MAYBE GOD JUTH HATH A WEIRD THENTH OF HUMOR.
1/29

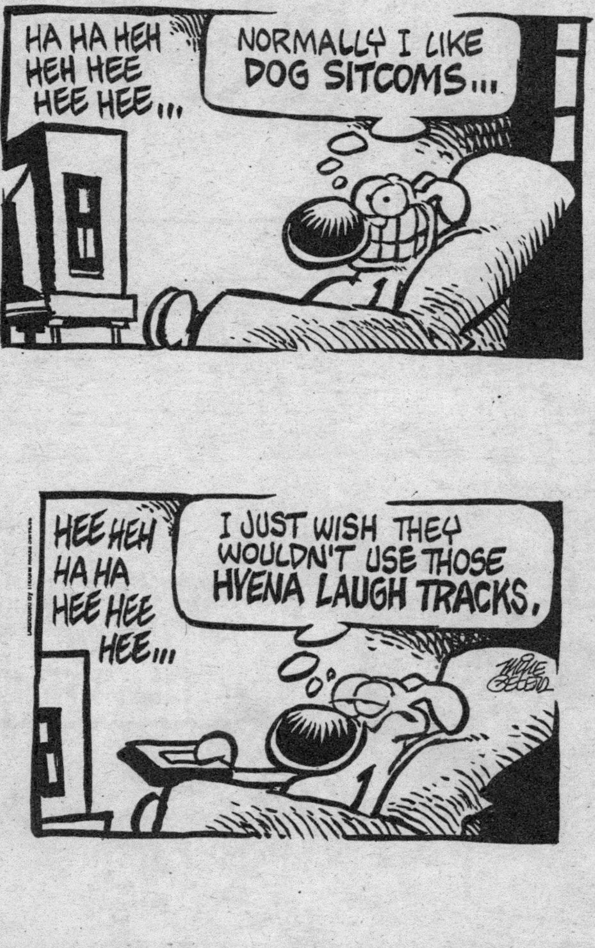
HA HA HEH HEH HEE HEE HEE...
NORMALLY I LIKE DOG SITCOMS...
HEE HEH HA HA HEE HEE HEE...
I JUST WISH THEY WOULDN'T USE THOSE HYENA LAUGH TRACKS.

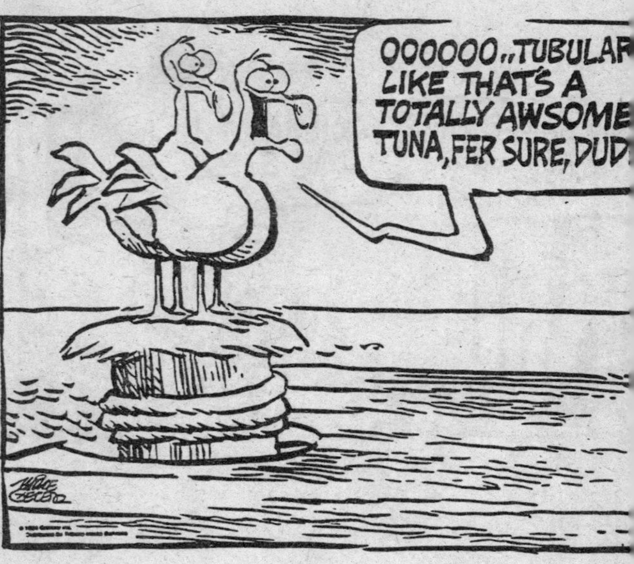
OOOOOO.,TUBULAR
LIKE THAT'S A
TOTALLY AWSOME
TUNA,FER SURE,DUD

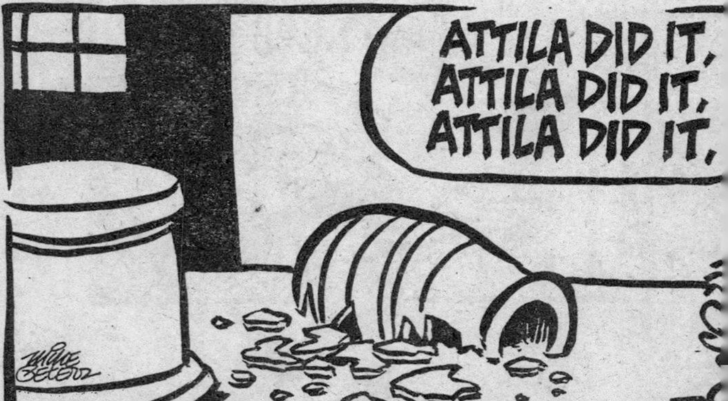
ATTILA DID IT,
ATTILA DID IT,
ATTILA DID IT,

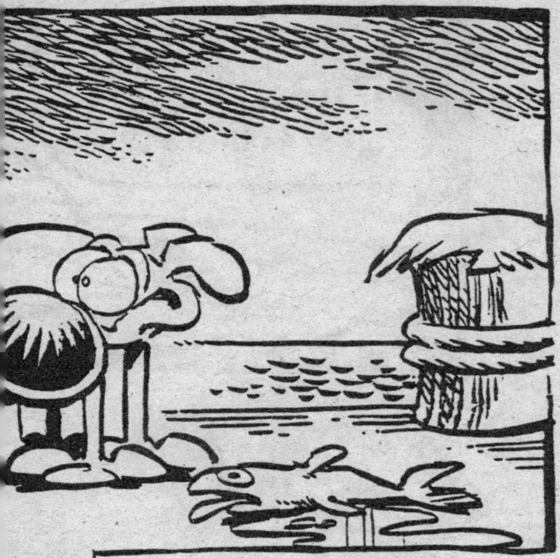

VALLEY GULLS

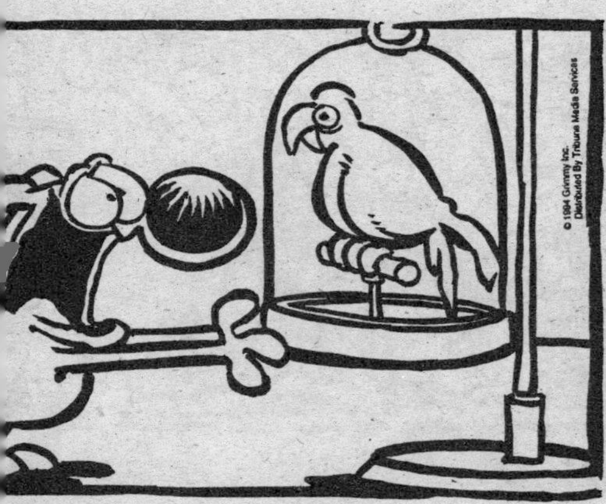
© 1994 Grimmy Inc.
Distributed By Tribune Media Services

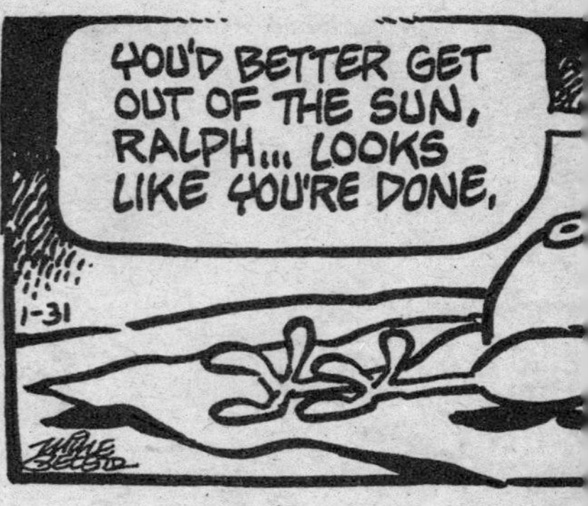
YOU'D BETTER GET OUT OF THE SUN, RALPH... LOOKS LIKE YOU'RE DONE.
1-31

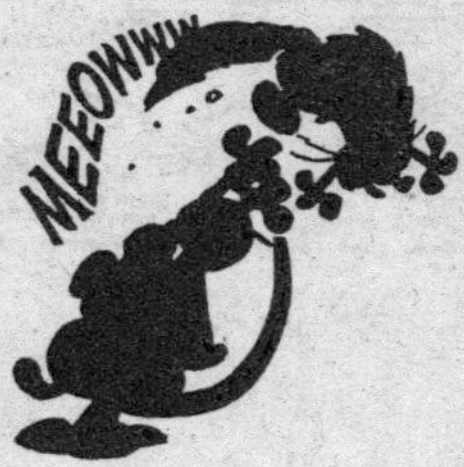
MEEOWWW

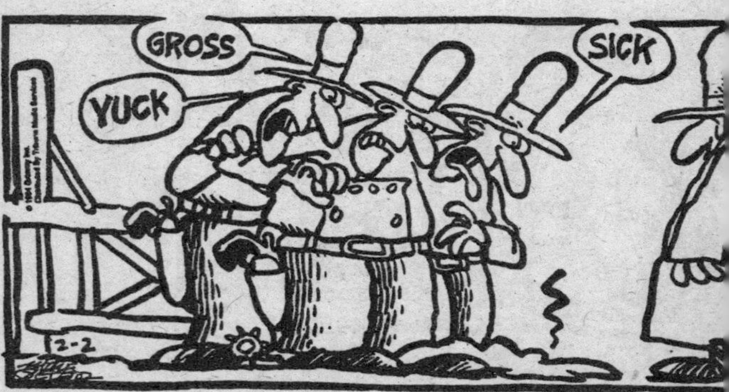
GROSS
YUCK
SICK
2-2

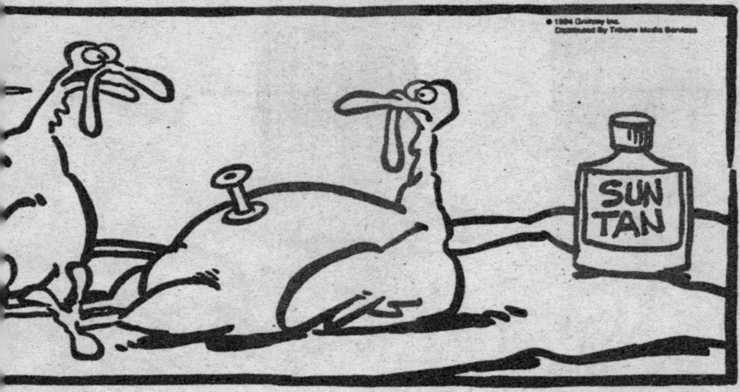
SUN
TAN

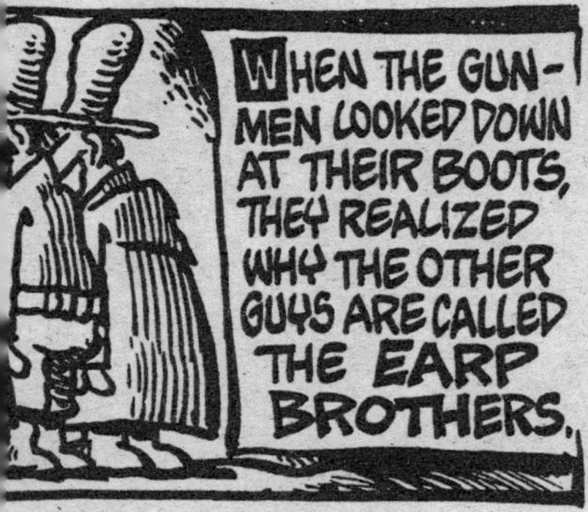
WHEN THE GUN-
MEN LOOKED DOWN
AT THEIR BOOTS,
THEY REALIZED
WHY THE OTHER
GUYS ARE CALLED
THE EARP
BROTHERS.

THIS SAYS THE GOVERNMENT DID RADIATION TESTING ON PEOPLE IN THE '50S AND '60S ...
SO THAT EXPLAINS THOSE GUYS IN THE 'WORLD WRESTLING FEDERATION.'
2/1

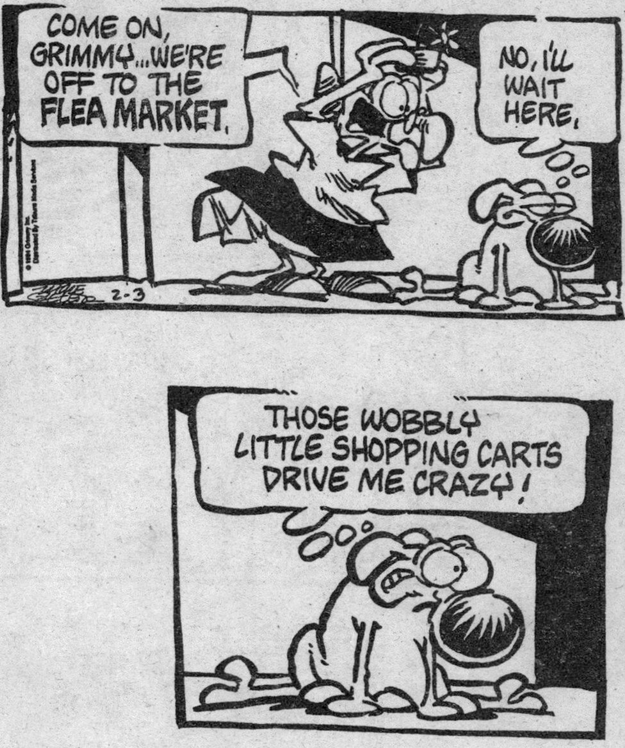
COME ON, GRIMMY...WE'RE OFF TO THE FLEA MARKET.
NO, I'LL WAIT HERE.
THOSE WOBBLY LITTLE SHOPPING CARTS DRIVE ME CRAZY!

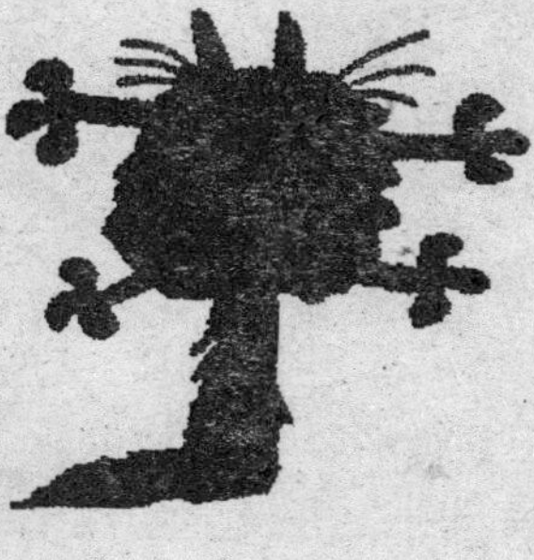

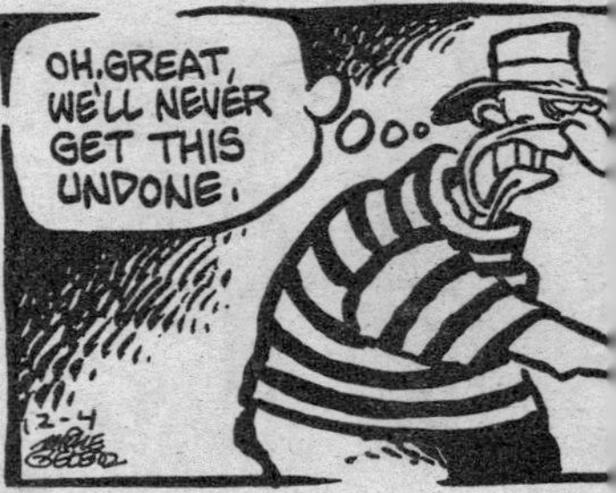
OH, GREAT, WE'LL NEVER GET THIS UNDONE.
Ooo
12-4

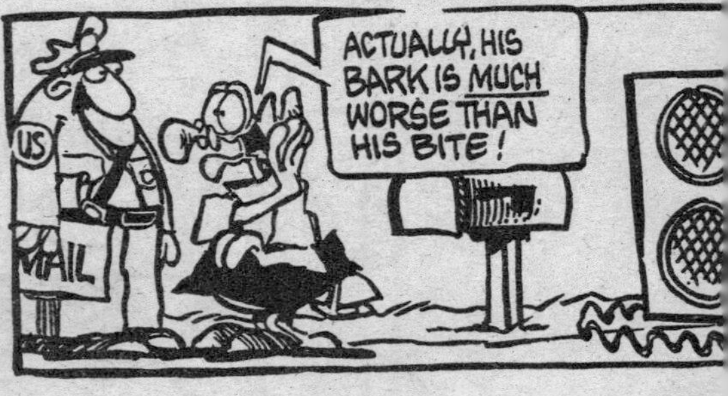
ACTUALLY, HIS BARK IS MUCH WORSE THAN HIS BITE!
US
MAIL

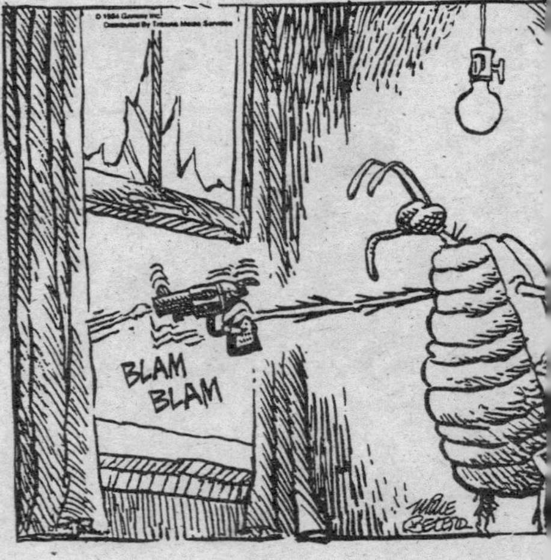
BLAM
BLAM

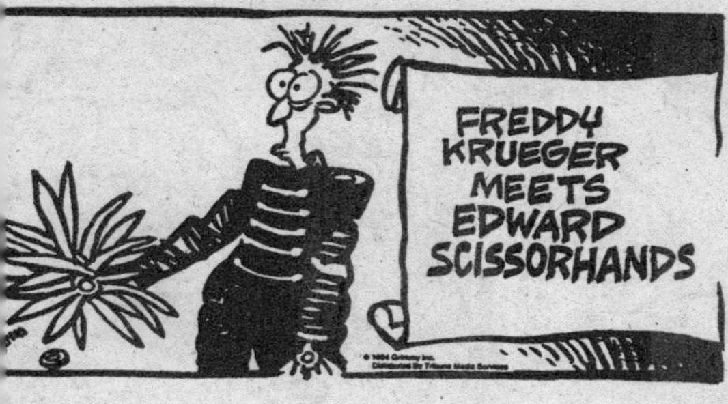
FREDDY KRUEGER MEETS EDWARD SCISSORHANDS

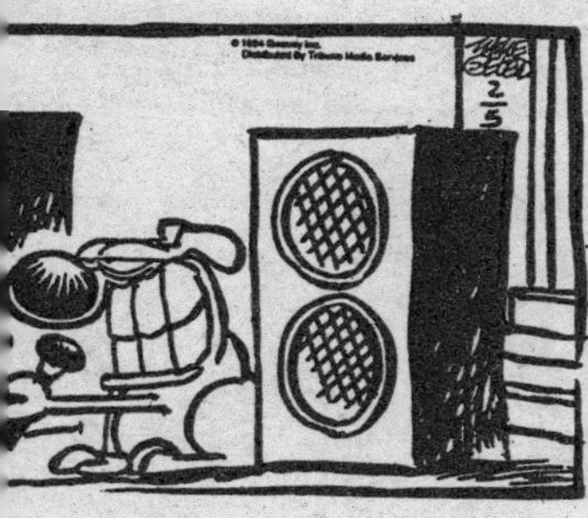
2/5

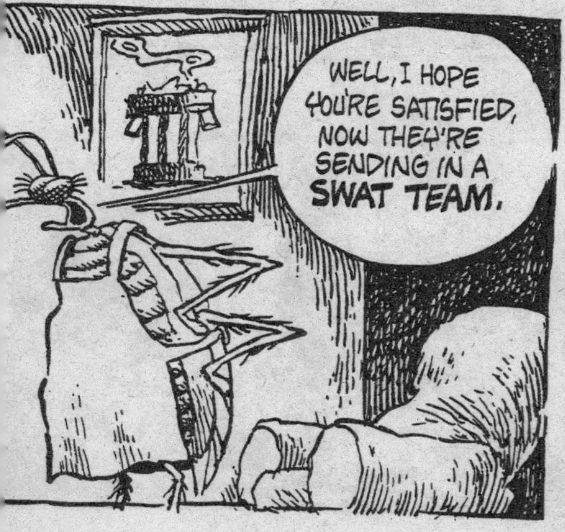
WELL, I HOPE YOU'RE SATISFIED, NOW THEY'RE SENDING IN A SWAT TEAM.

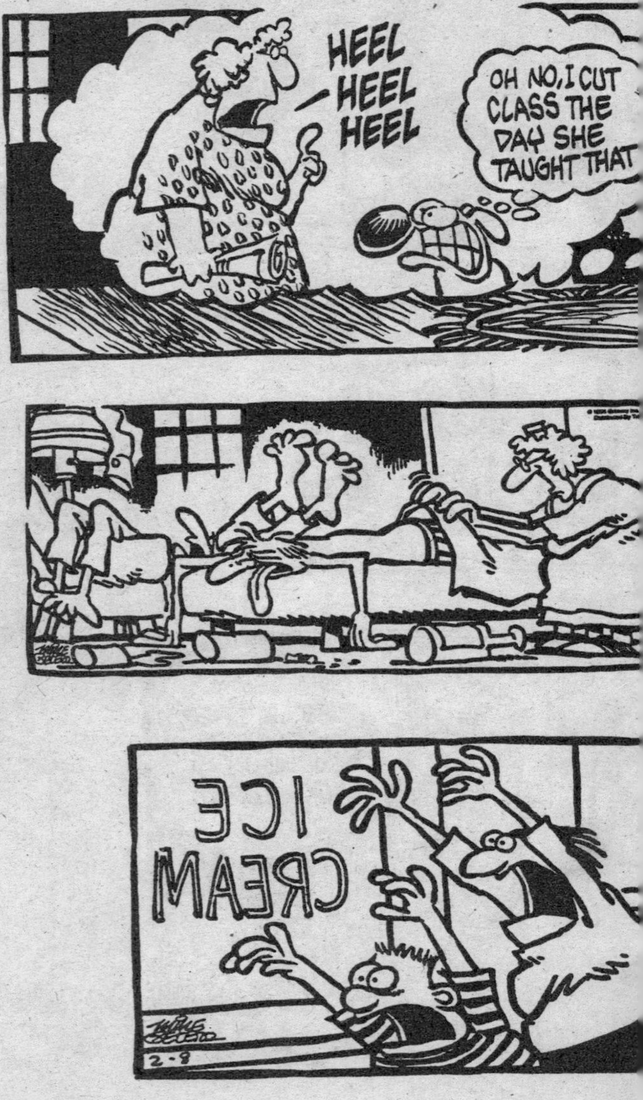
HEEL
HEEL
HEEL
OH NO, I CUT CLASS THE DAY SHE TAUGHT THAT
ICE CREAM
2-8

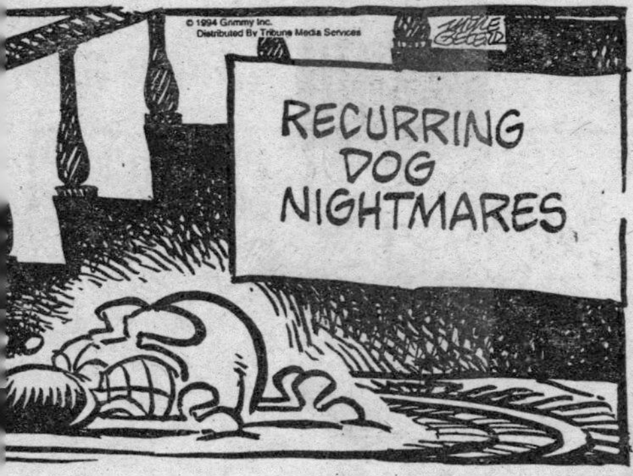
© 1994 Grimmy Inc.
Distributed By Tribune Media Services
RECURRING DOG NIGHTMARES

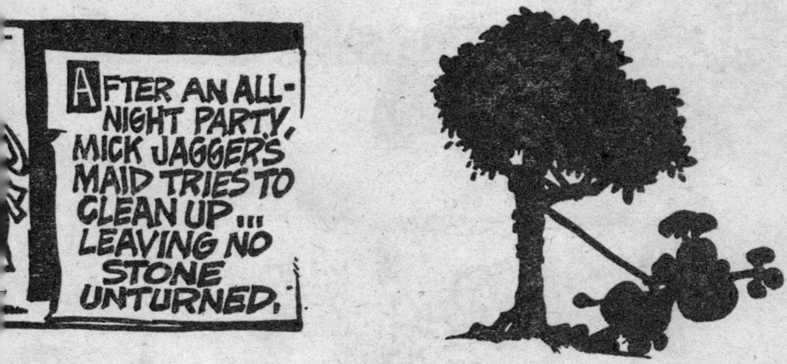
AFTER AN ALL-NIGHT PARTY, MICK JAGGER'S MAID TRIES TO CLEAN UP... LEAVING NO STONE UNTURNED.

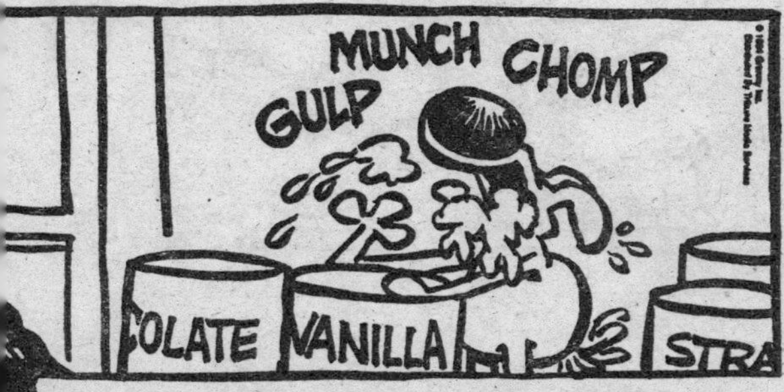
MUNCH
CHOMP
GULP
OLATE
VANILLA
STRA

HOUND OF THE BASKIN-ROBBINS

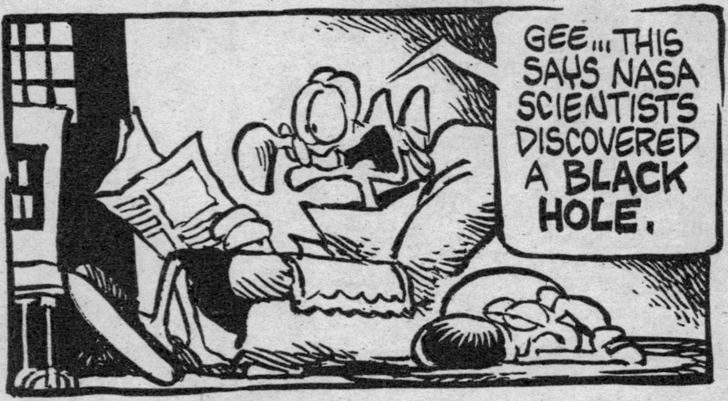
GEE... THIS SAYS NASA SCIENTISTS DISCOVERED A BLACK HOLE.

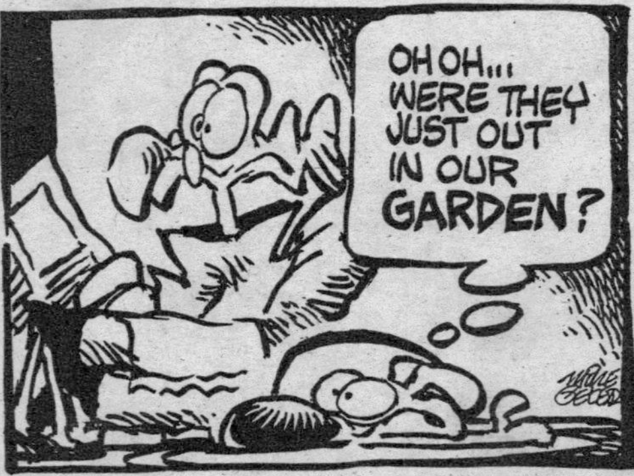
OH OH... WERE THEY JUST OUT IN OUR GARDEN?

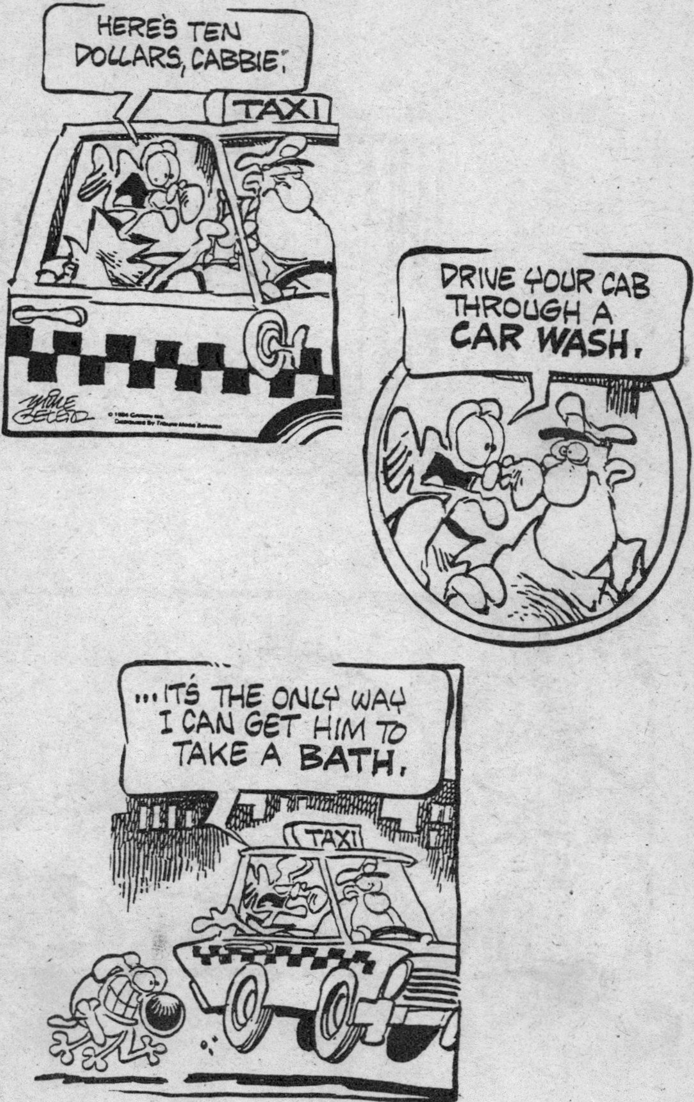
HERE'S TEN DOLLARS, CABBIE.
TAXI
DRIVE YOUR CAB THROUGH A CAR WASH.
...IT'S THE ONLY WAY I CAN GET HIM TO TAKE A BATH.
TAXI

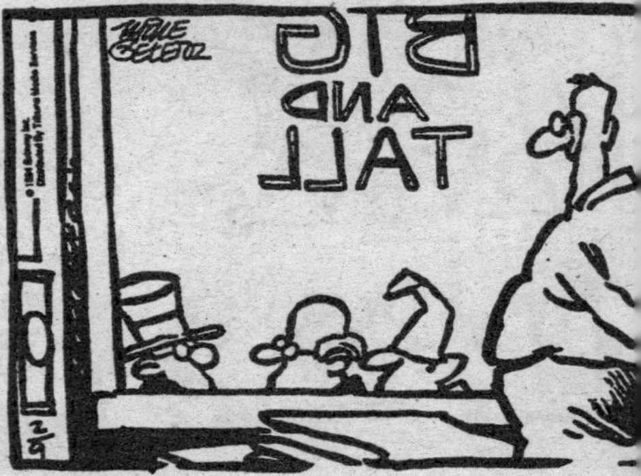
BIG
AND
TALL

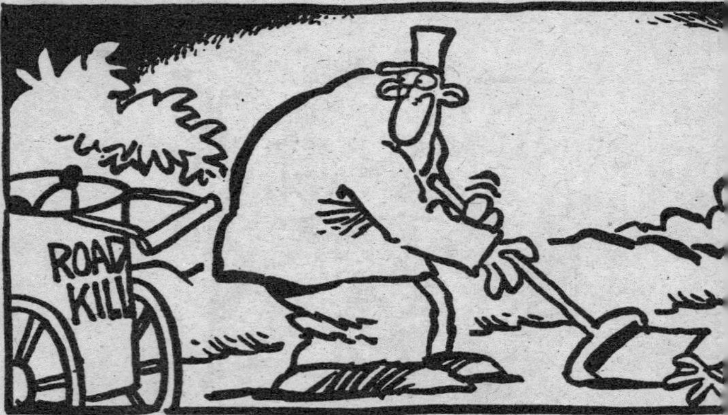
ROAD
KILL

EVENTUALLY, CARL DECIDED TO MOVE HIS BIG AND TALL STORE OUT OF OZ...

SECRETLY, BEFORE THE GATES OPEN, THE DISNEYLAND HIGHWAY CLEAN-UP CREW GOES ABOUT ITS UGLY BUSINESS...

2-10 © 1994 Disney Inc. Distributed By Tribune Media Services

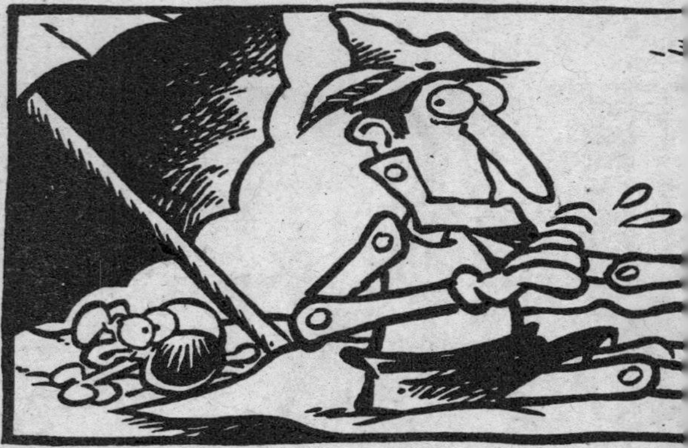

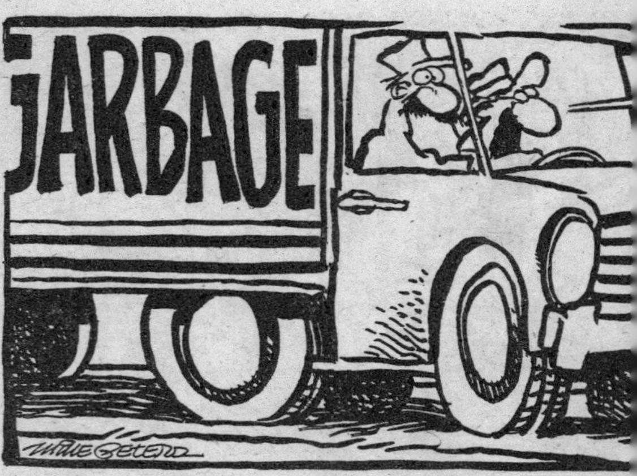
GARBAGE

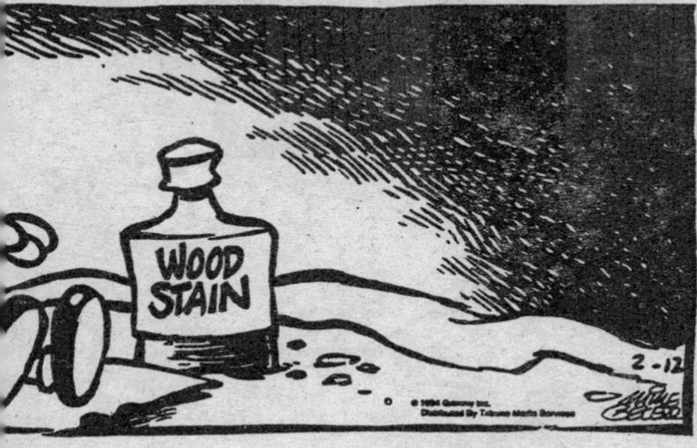
WOOD STAIN
2-12

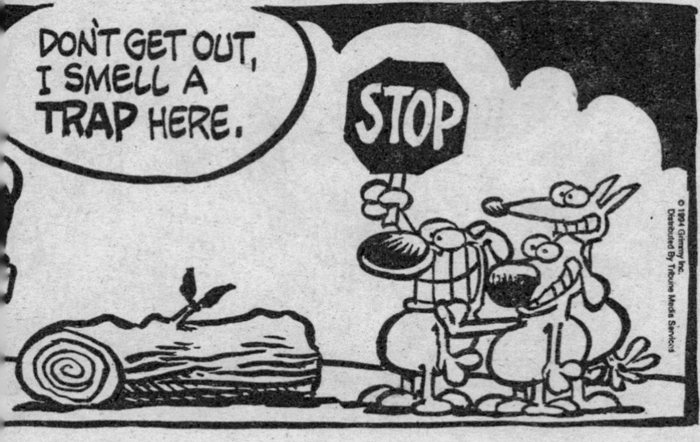
DON'T GET OUT, I SMELL A TRAP HERE.
STOP
© 1994 Grimmy Inc.
Distributed By Tribune Media Services

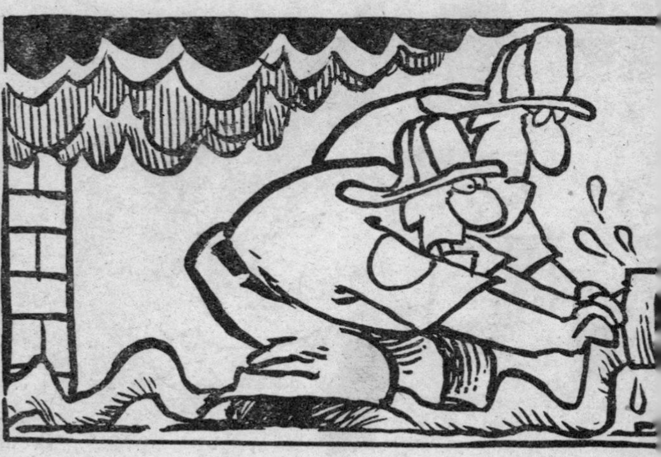

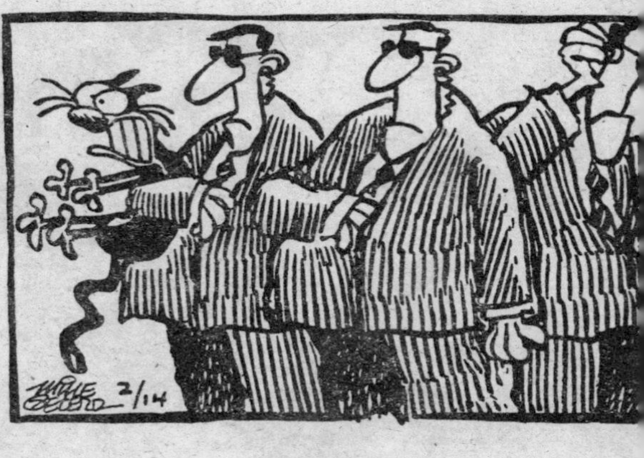
2/14

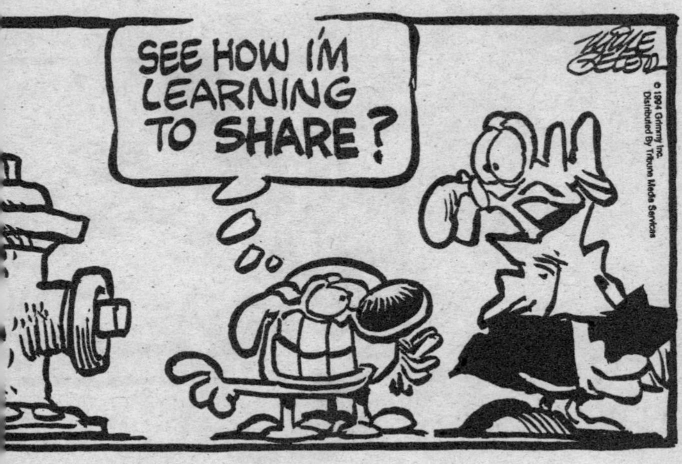
SEE HOW I'M LEARNING TO SHARE?
© 1984 Grimmy Inc.
Distributed By Tribune Media Services

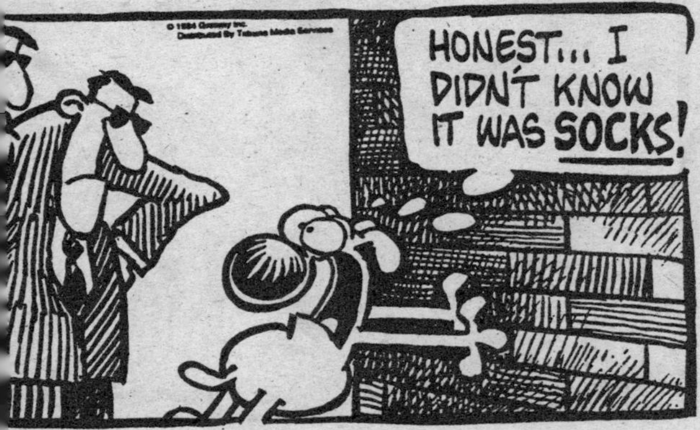
HONEST... I DIDN'T KNOW IT WAS SOCKS!

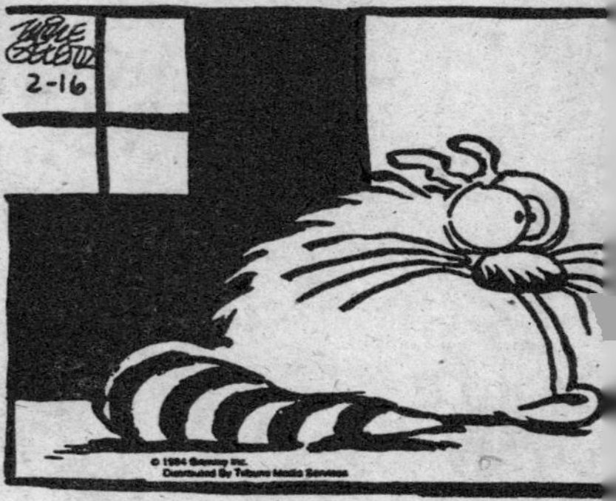
2-16

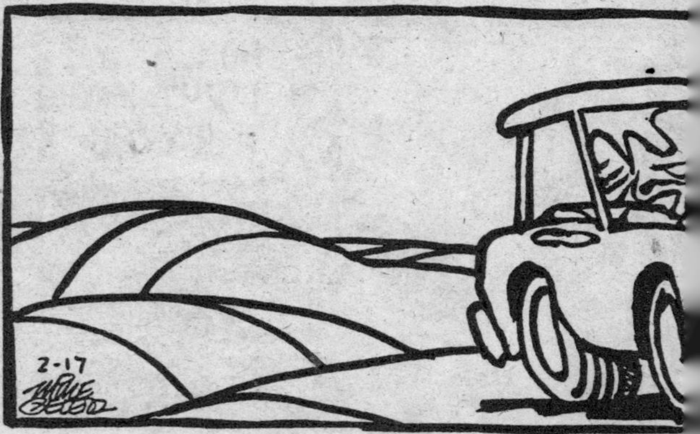
2-17

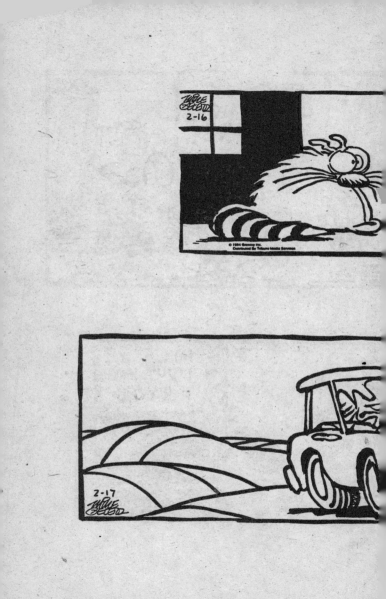

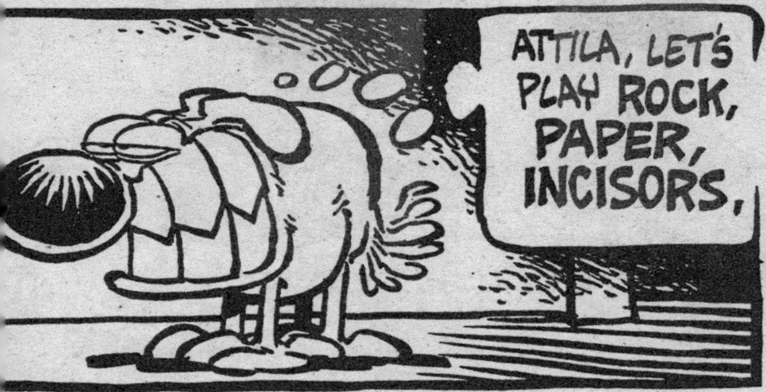
ATTILA, LET'S PLAY ROCK, PAPER, INCISORS.

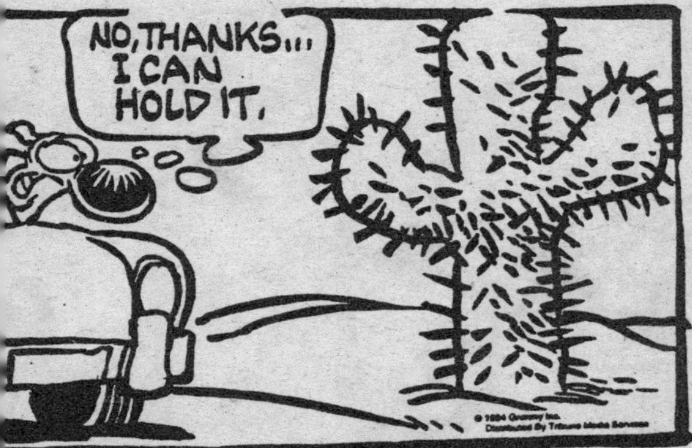
NO, THANKS... I CAN HOLD IT.

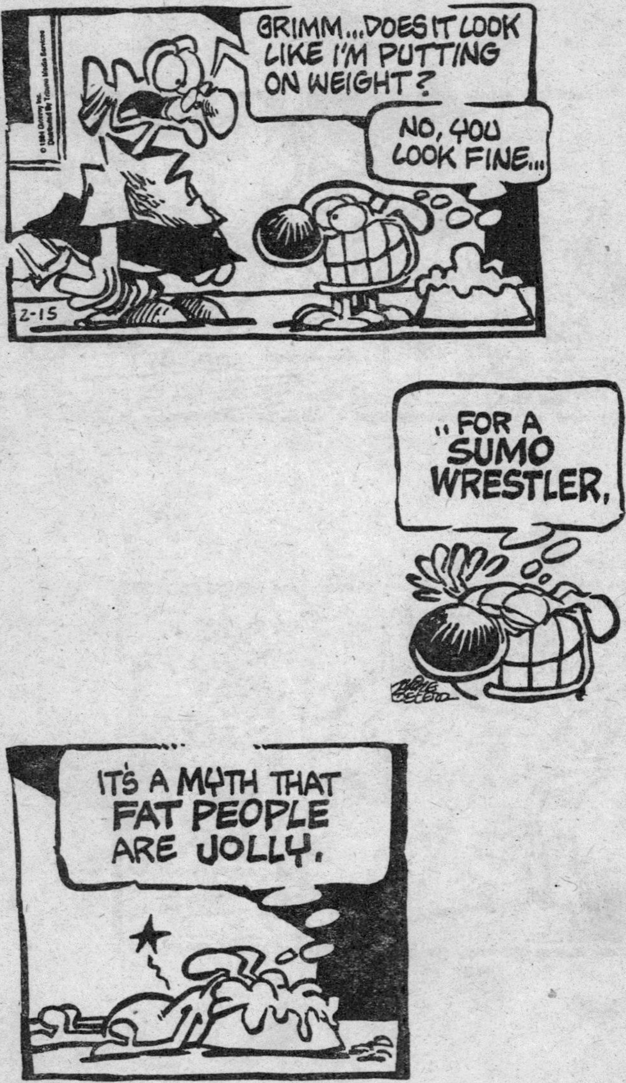
GRIMM...DOES IT LOOK LIKE I'M PUTTING ON WEIGHT?
NO, YOU LOOK FINE...
2-15
..FOR A SUMO WRESTLER.
IT'S A MYTH THAT FAT PEOPLE ARE JOLLY.

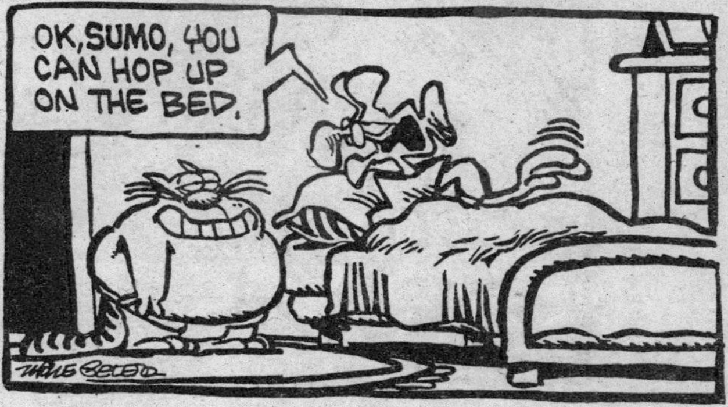
OK, SUMO, YOU CAN HOP UP ON THE BED.

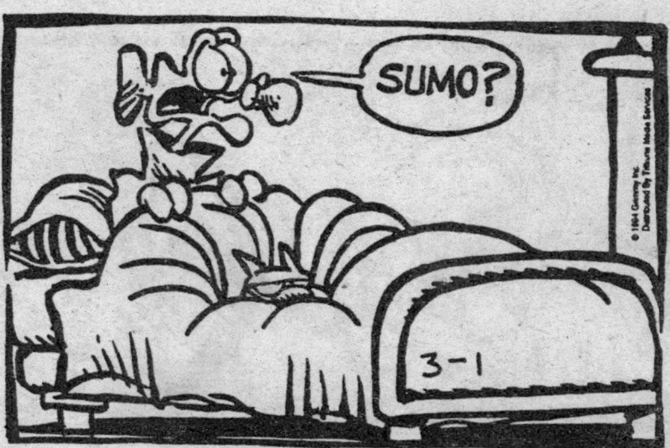
SUMO?
© 1984 Grimmy Inc. Distributed By Tribune Media Services
3-1

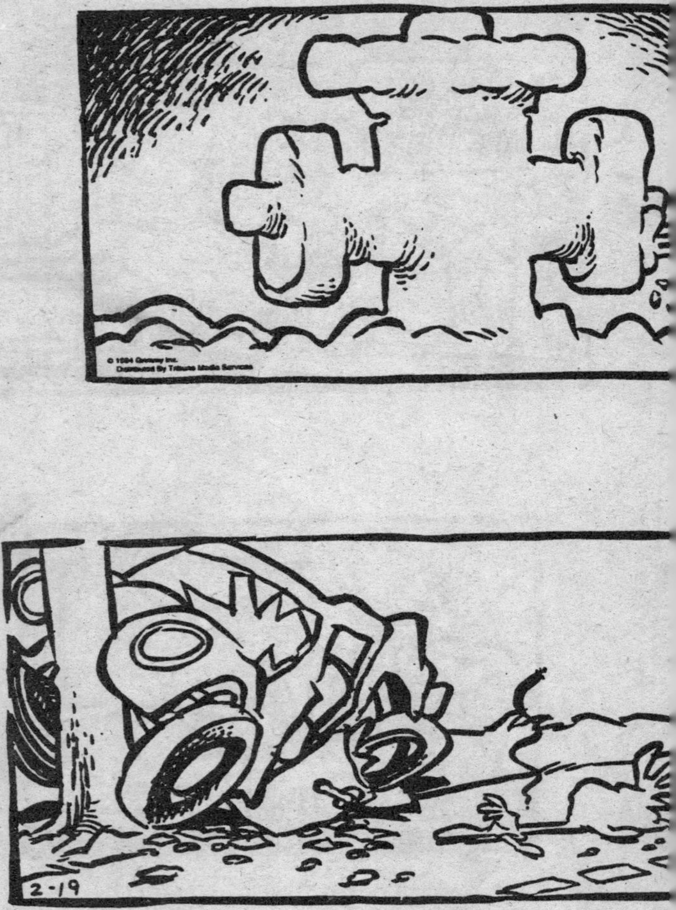
2-19

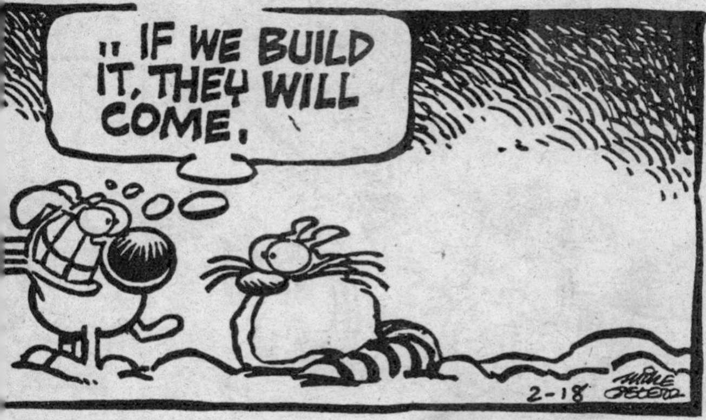
.. IF WE BUILD IT, THEY WILL COME.
2-18

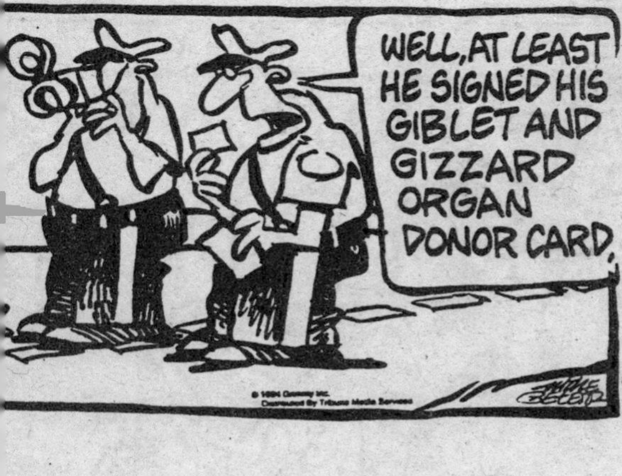
WELL, AT LEAST HE SIGNED HIS GIBLET AND GIZZARD ORGAN DONOR CARD.

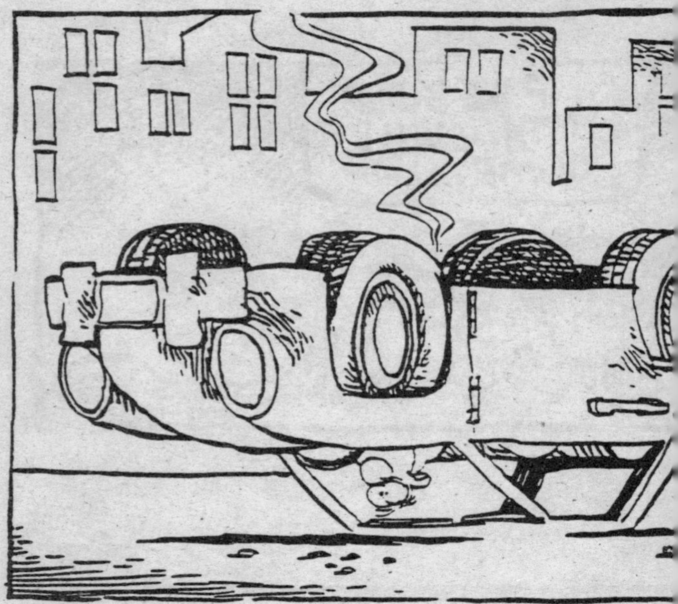

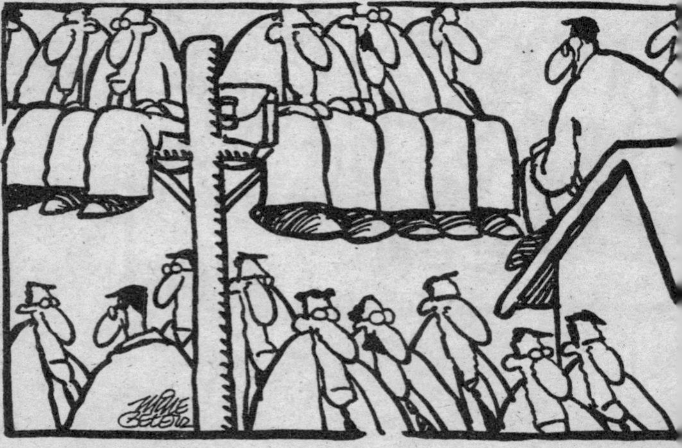

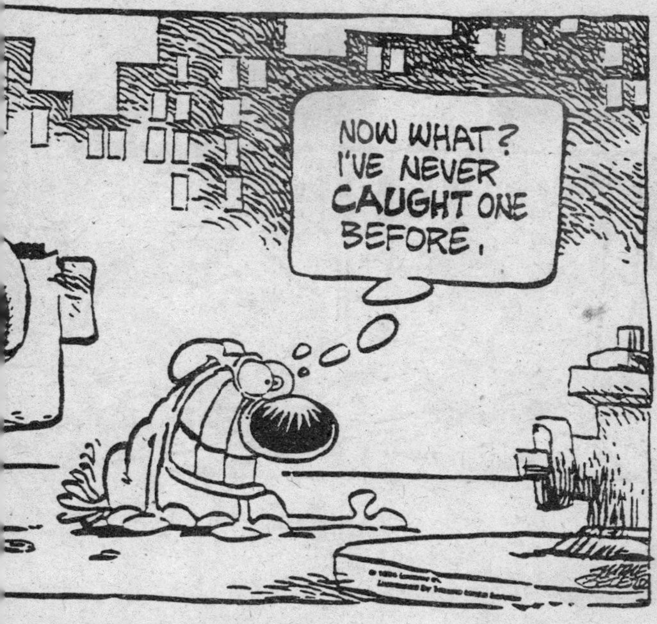
NOW WHAT? I'VE NEVER CAUGHT ONE BEFORE.

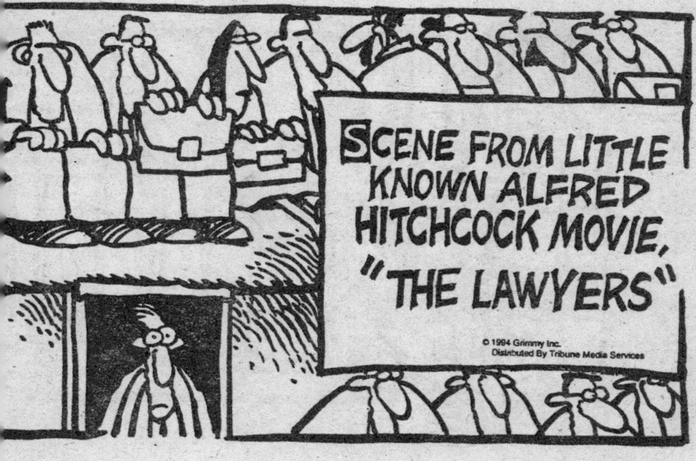
SCENE FROM LITTLE KNOWN ALFRED HITCHCOCK MOVIE, "THE LAWYERS"
© 1994 Grimmy Inc. Distributed By Tribune Media Services

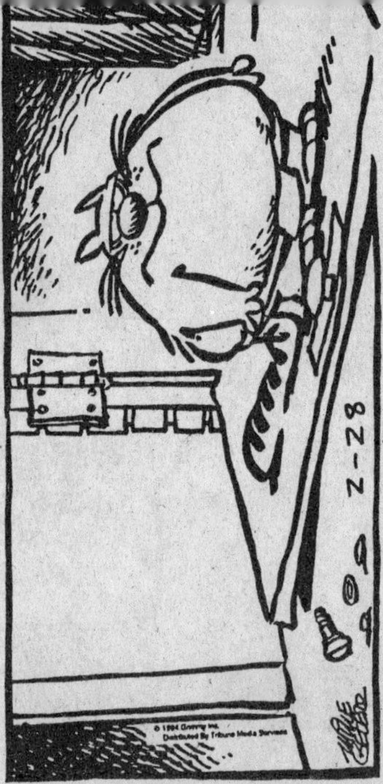
2-28
Distributed By Tribune Media Services

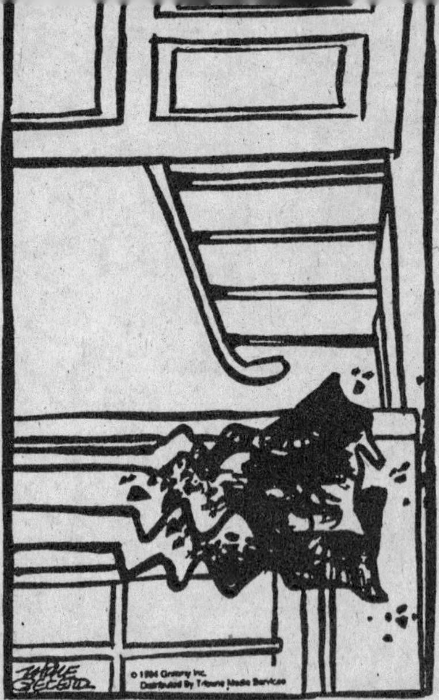
Distributed By Tribune Media Services

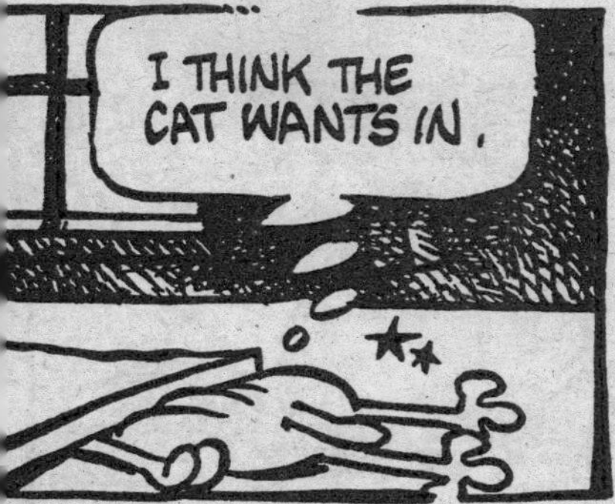
I THINK THE CAT WANTS IN.

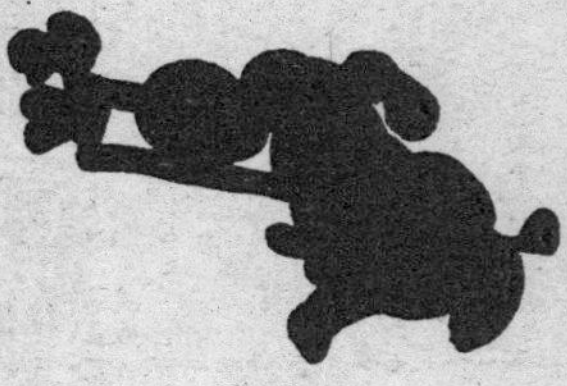

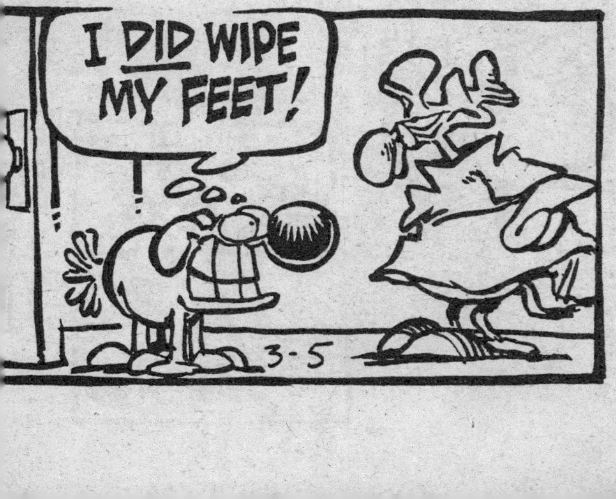
I DID WIPE MY FEET!
3-5

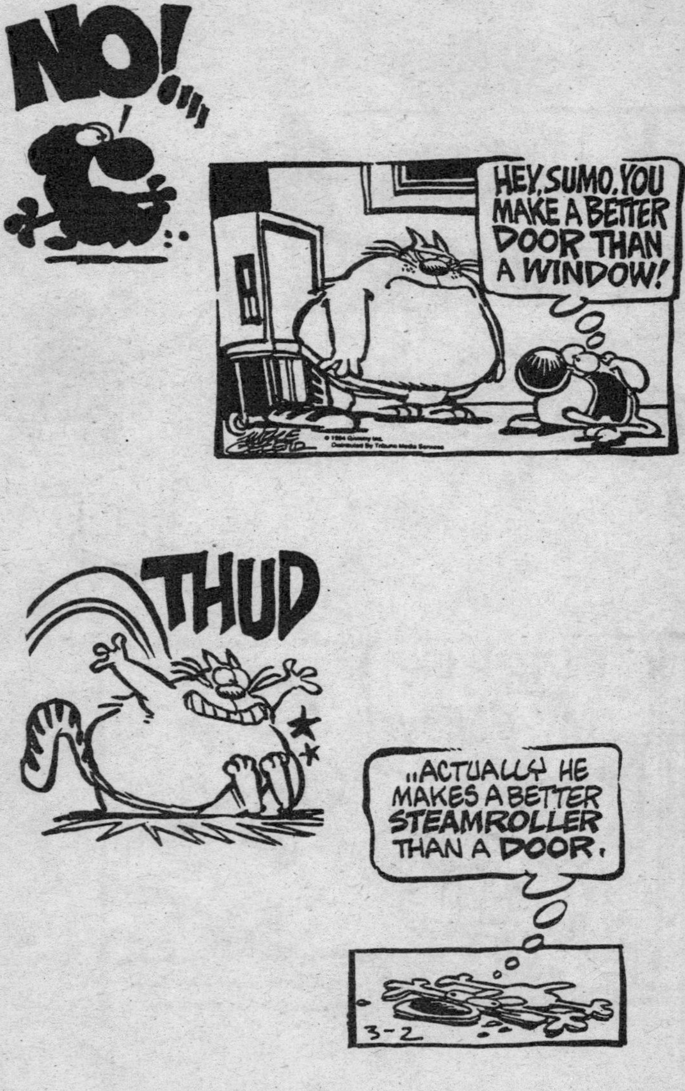
NO!
HEY, SUMO. YOU MAKE A BETTER DOOR THAN A WINDOW!
THUD
..ACTUALLY HE MAKES A BETTER STEAMROLLER THAN A DOOR.
3-2

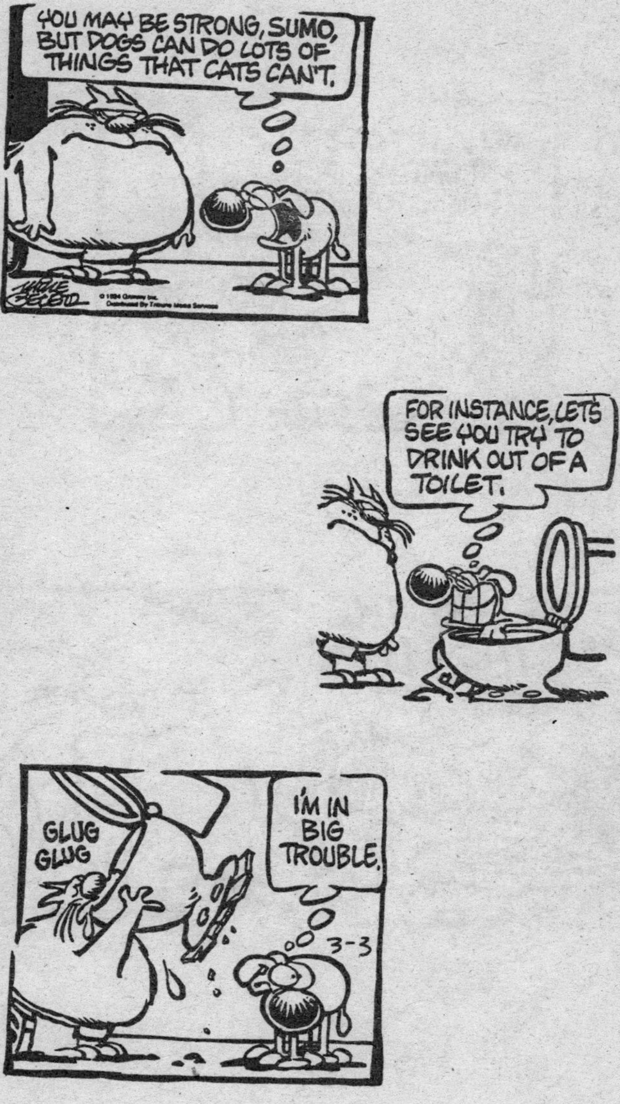
YOU MAY BE STRONG, SUMO, BUT DOGS CAN DO LOTS OF THINGS THAT CATS CAN'T.
FOR INSTANCE, LET'S SEE YOU TRY TO DRINK OUT OF A TOILET.
GLUG GLUG
I'M IN BIG TROUBLE.
3-3

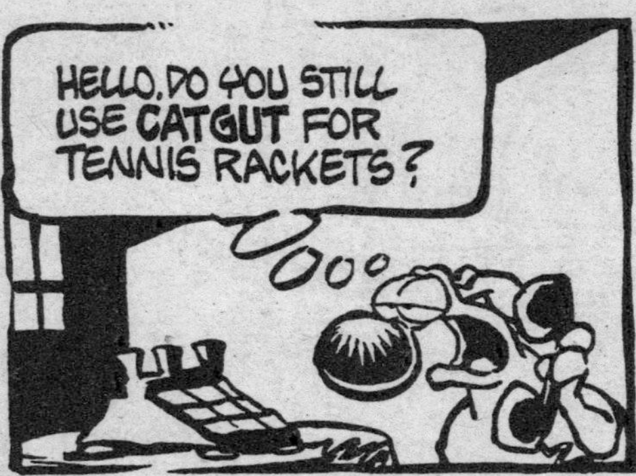
HELLO, DO YOU STILL USE CATGUT FOR TENNIS RACKETS?

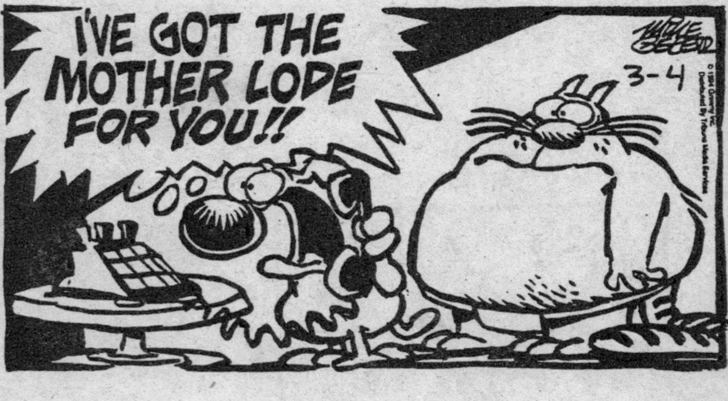
I'VE GOT THE MOTHER LODE FOR YOU!!
3-4
© 1994 Grimmy Inc.
Distributed By Tribune Media Services

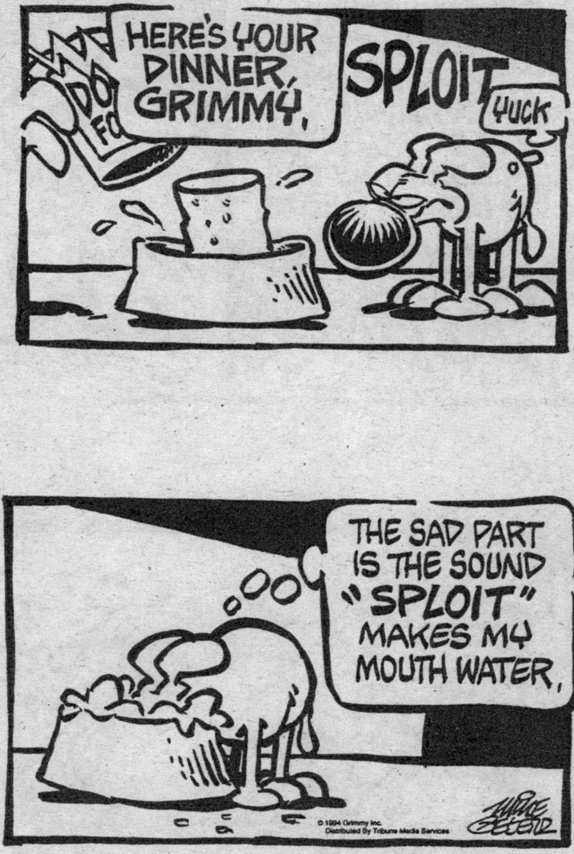
HERE'S YOUR DINNER, GRIMMY.
SPLOIT
YUCK
THE SAD PART IS THE SOUND "SPLOIT" MAKES MY MOUTH WATER.
© 1994 Grimmy Inc. Distributed By Tribune Media Services

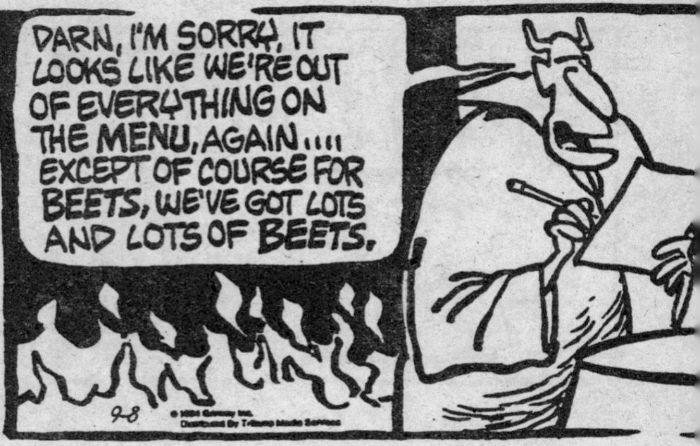
DARN, I'M SORRY, IT LOOKS LIKE WE'RE OUT OF EVERYTHING ON THE MENU, AGAIN.... EXCEPT OF COURSE FOR BEETS, WE'VE GOT LOTS AND LOTS OF BEETS.
9-8

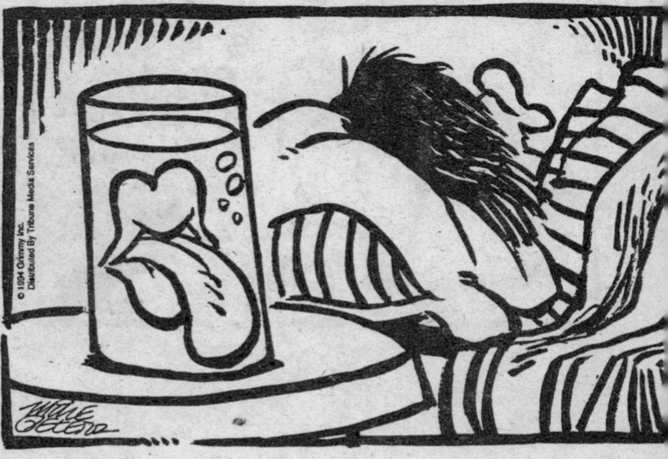
© 1994 Grimmy Inc.
Distributed By Tribune Media Services

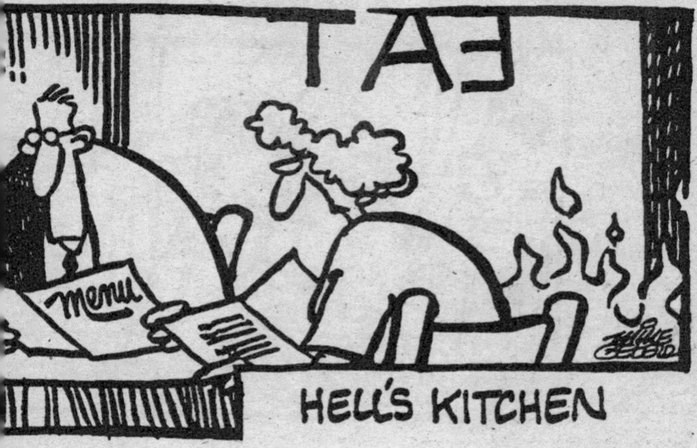
EAT
menu

HELL'S KITCHEN

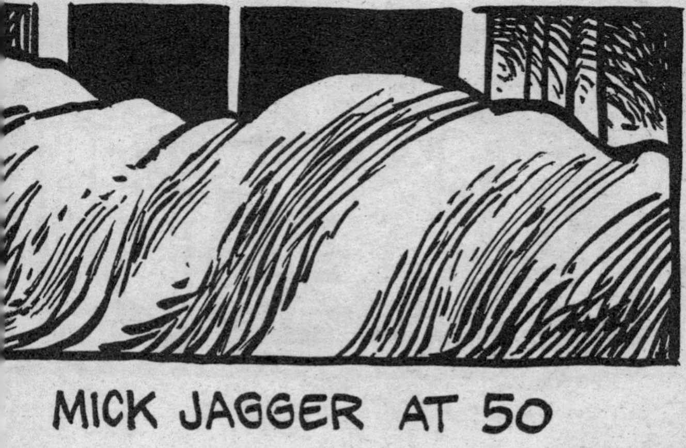

MICK JAGGER AT 50

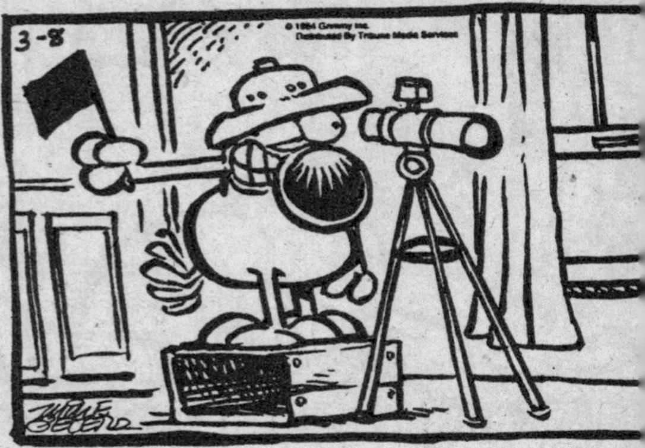
3-8
© 1994 Grimmy Inc.
Distributed By Tribune Media Services

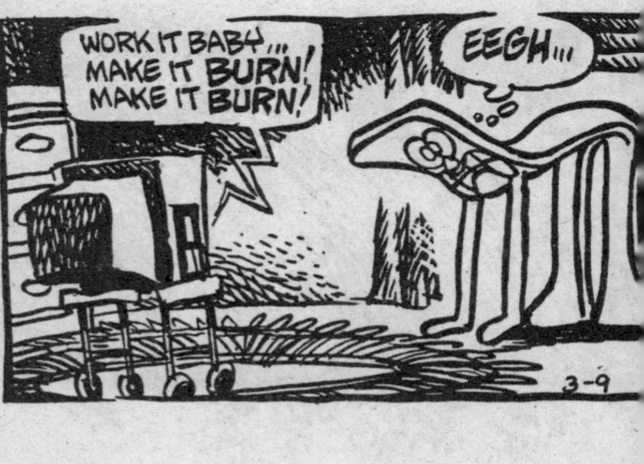
WORK IT BABY... MAKE IT BURN! MAKE IT BURN!
EEGH...
3-9

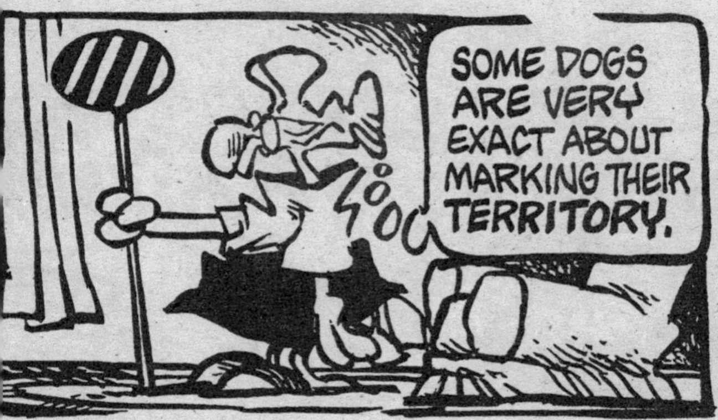
SOME DOGS ARE VERY EXACT ABOUT MARKING THEIR TERRITORY.

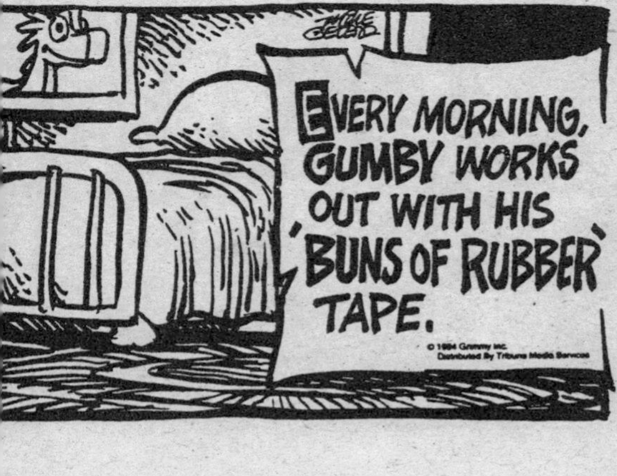
EVERY MORNING, GUMBY WORKS OUT WITH HIS 'BUNS OF RUBBER' TAPE.
© 1994 Grimmy Inc.
Distributed By Tribune Media Services

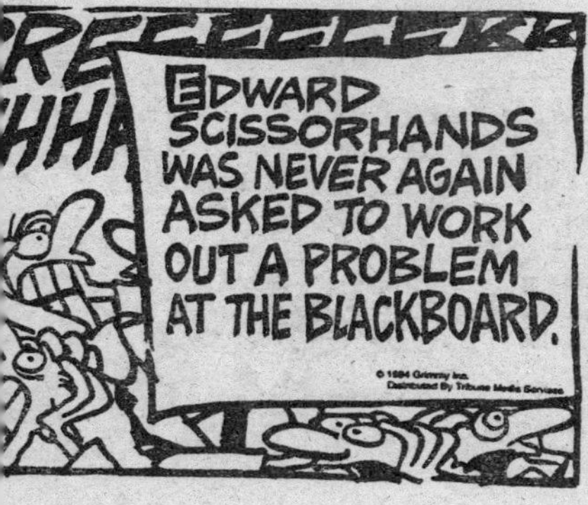
EDWARD SCISSORHANDS WAS NEVER AGAIN ASKED TO WORK OUT A PROBLEM AT THE BLACKBOARD.
© 1994 Grimmy Inc.
Distributed By Tribune Media Services

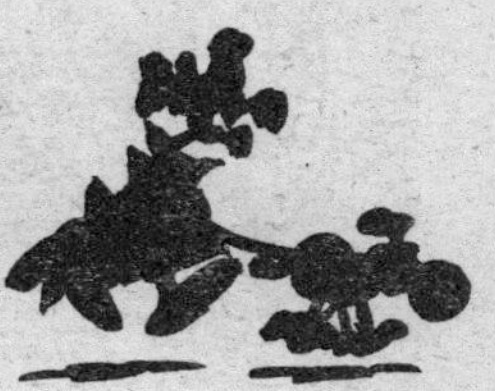

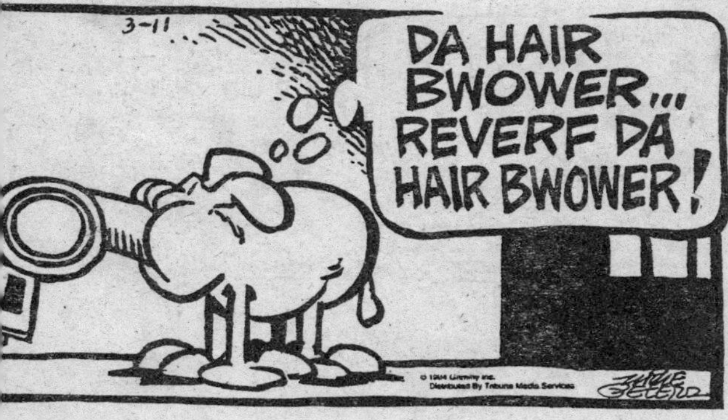
3-11
DA HAIR BWOWER... REVERF DA HAIR BWOWER!
© 1994 Grimmy Inc.
Distributed By Tribune Media Services

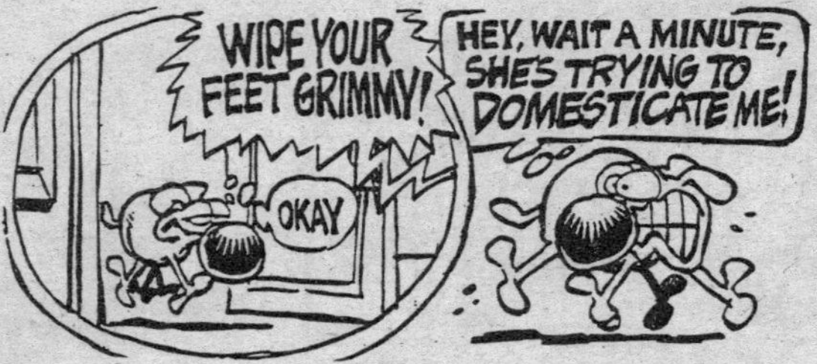
WIPE YOUR FEET GRIMMY!
OKAY
HEY, WAIT A MINUTE, SHE'S TRYING TO DOMESTICATE ME!

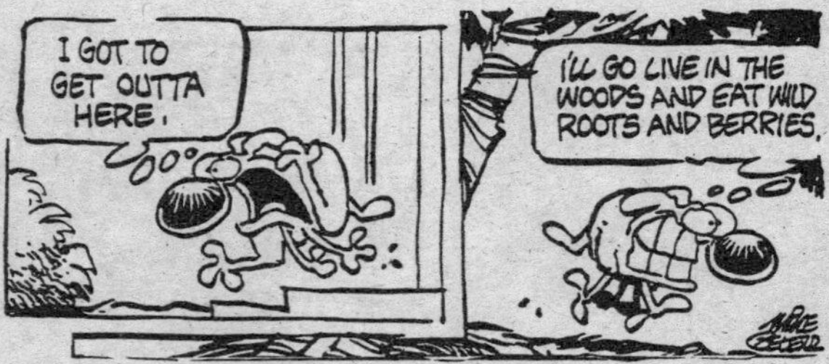
I GOT TO GET OUTTA HERE.
I'LL GO LIVE IN THE WOODS AND EAT WILD ROOTS AND BERRIES.

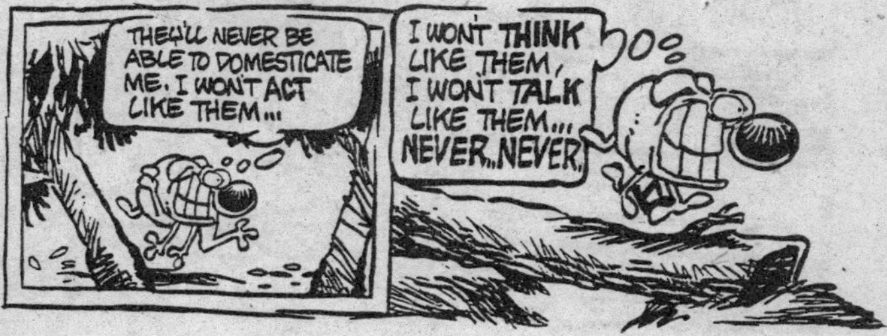
THEY'LL NEVER BE ABLE TO DOMESTICATE ME. I WON'T ACT LIKE THEM...
I WON'T THINK LIKE THEM, I WON'T TALK LIKE THEM... NEVER..NEVER,

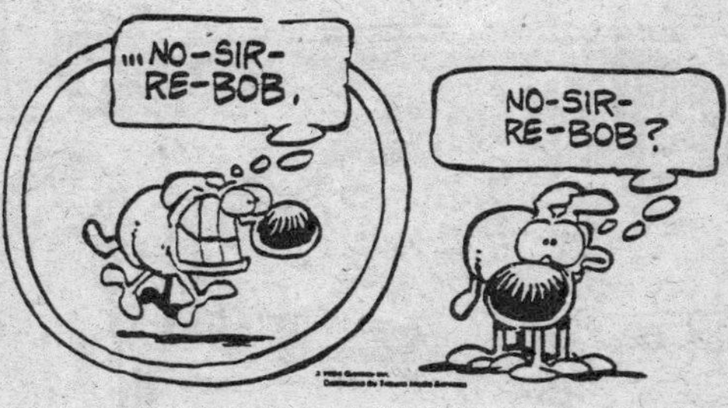
...NO-SIR-RE-BOB.
NO-SIR-RE-BOB?

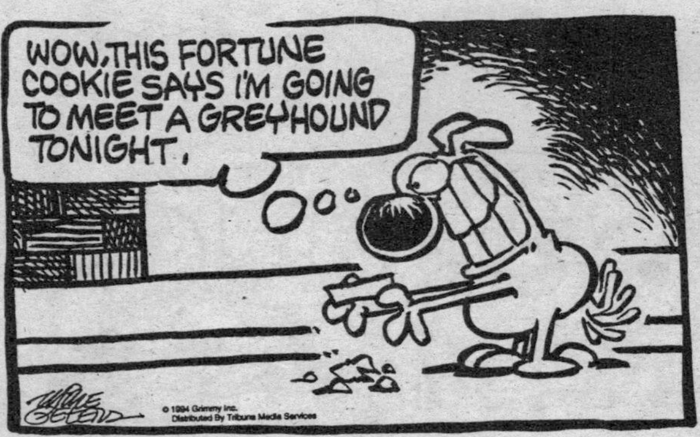
WOW, THIS FORTUNE COOKIE SAYS I'M GOING TO MEET A GREYHOUND TONIGHT.
© 1994 Grimmy Inc.
Distributed By Tribune Media Services

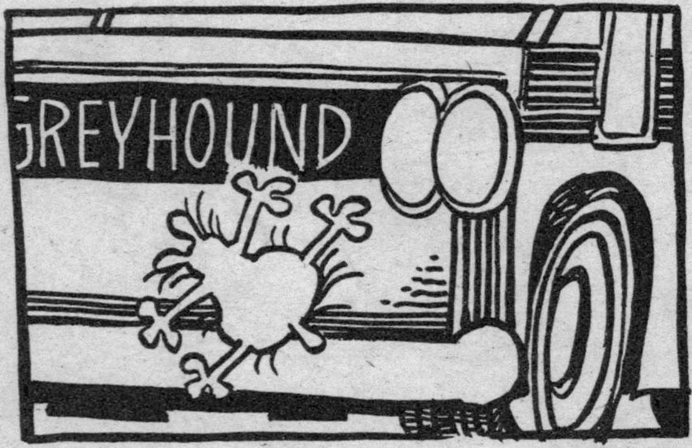
GREYHOUND

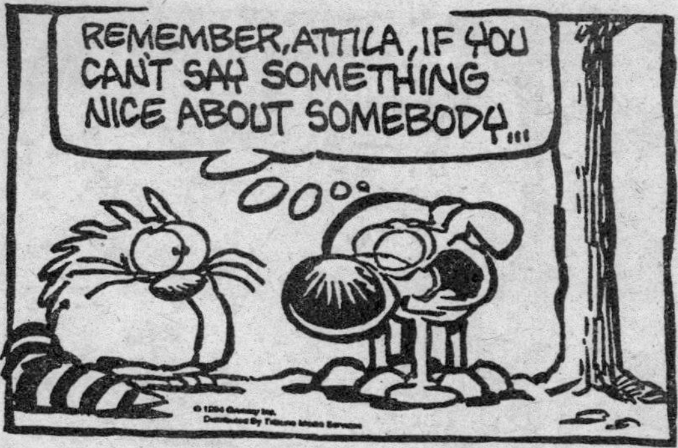
REMEMBER, ATTILA, IF YOU CAN'T SAY SOMETHING NICE ABOUT SOMEBODY...

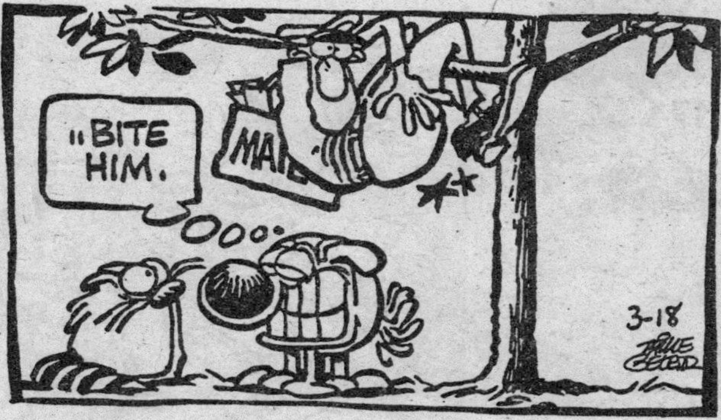
...BITE HIM.
3-18

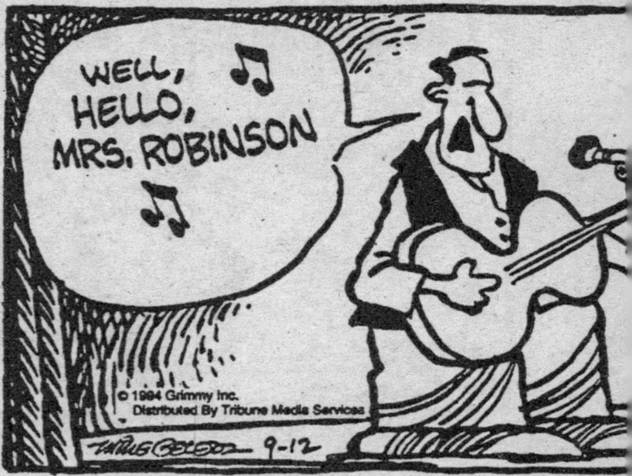
WELL, HELLO, MRS. ROBINSON
© 1994 Grimmy Inc.
Distributed By Tribune Media Services
9-12

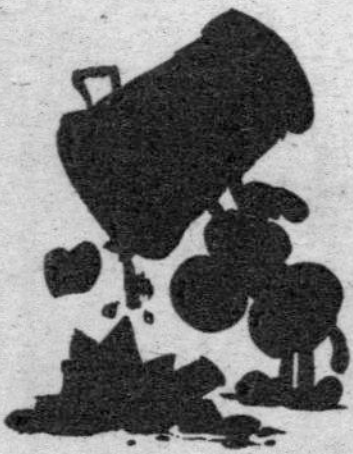

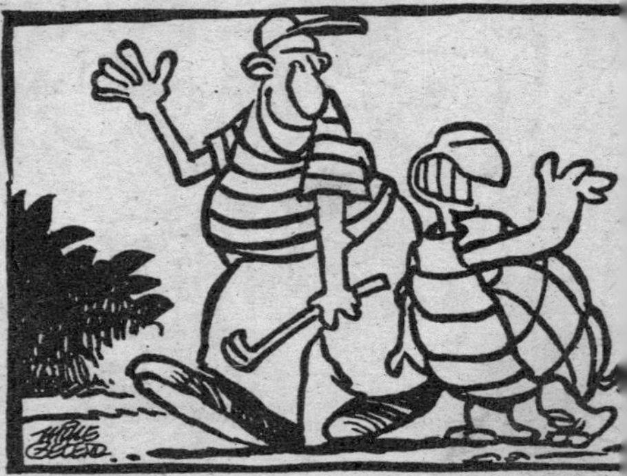

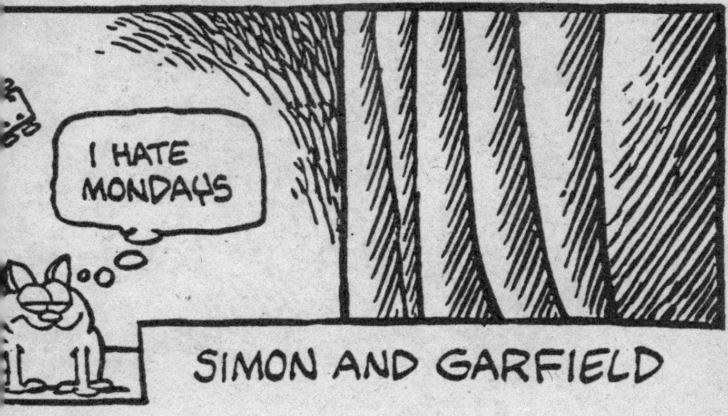
I HATE MONDAYS
SIMON AND GARFIELD

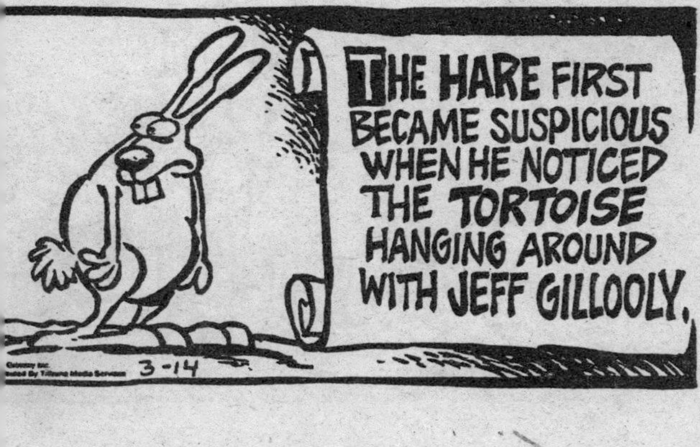
THE HARE FIRST BECAME SUSPICIOUS WHEN HE NOTICED THE TORTOISE HANGING AROUND WITH JEFF GILLOOLY.
3-14

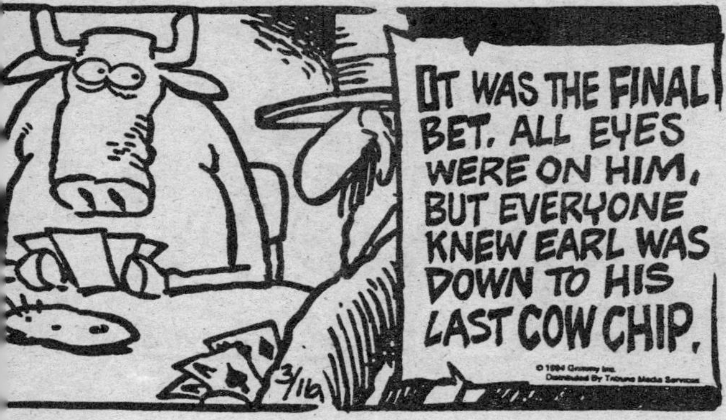
IT WAS THE FINAL BET. ALL EYES WERE ON HIM, BUT EVERYONE KNEW EARL WAS DOWN TO HIS LAST COW CHIP.
3/16
© 1994 Grimmy Inc.
Distributed By Tribune Media Services

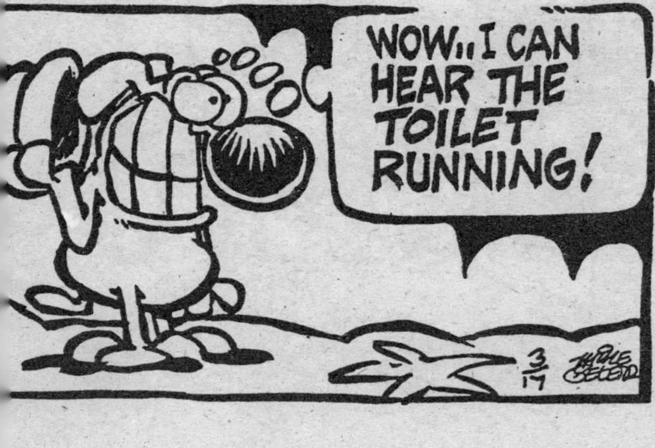
WOW.. I CAN HEAR THE TOILET RUNNING!
3/17

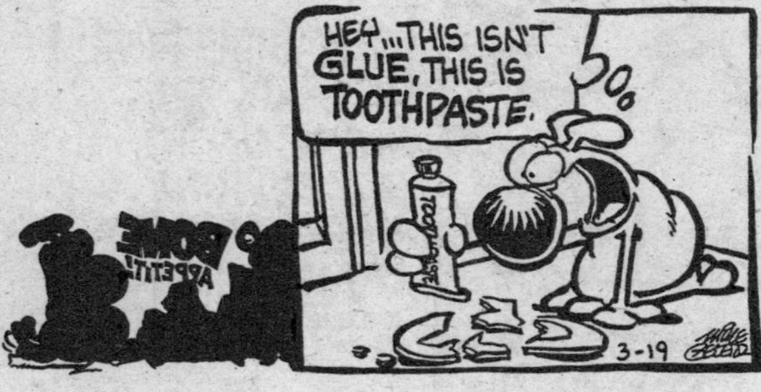
HEY...THIS ISN'T GLUE, THIS IS TOOTHPASTE.
3-19

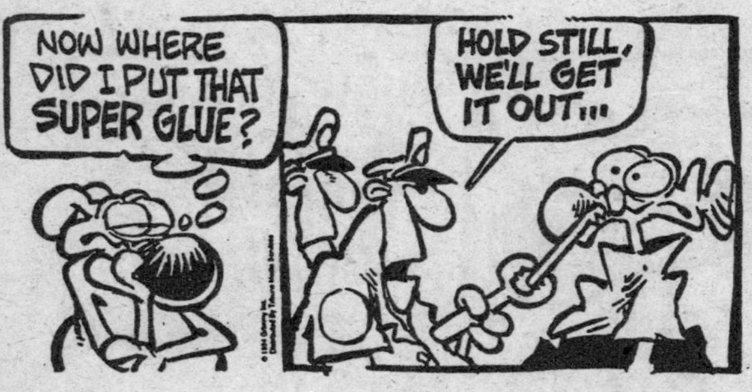
NOW WHERE DID I PUT THAT SUPER GLUE?
HOLD STILL, WE'LL GET IT OUT...

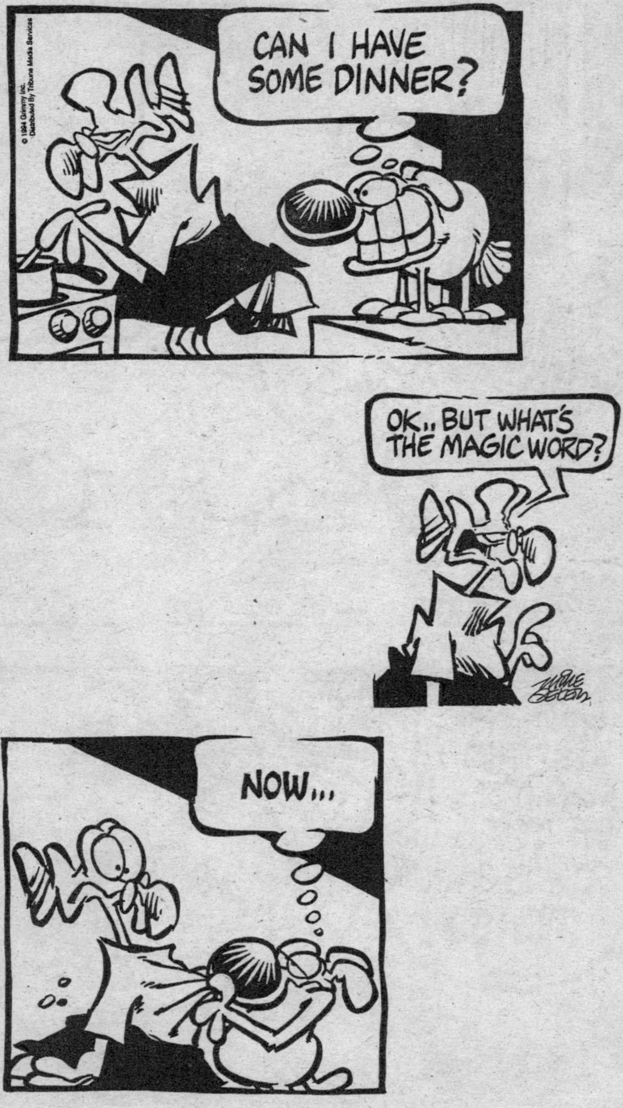
© 1994 Grimmy Inc. Distributed By Tribune Media Services
CAN I HAVE SOME DINNER?
OK,, BUT WHAT'S THE MAGIC WORD?
NOW...

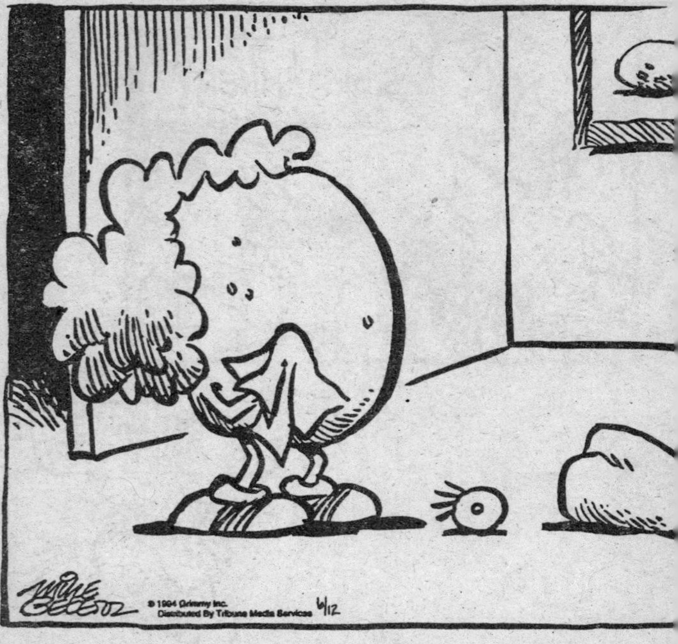
© 1994 Grimmy Inc.
Distributed By Tribune Media Services 6/12

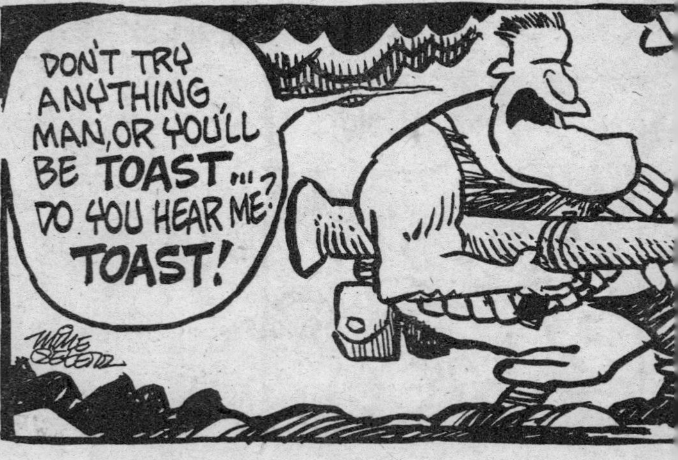
DON'T TRY ANYTHING, MAN, OR YOU'LL BE TOAST... DO YOU HEAR ME? TOAST!

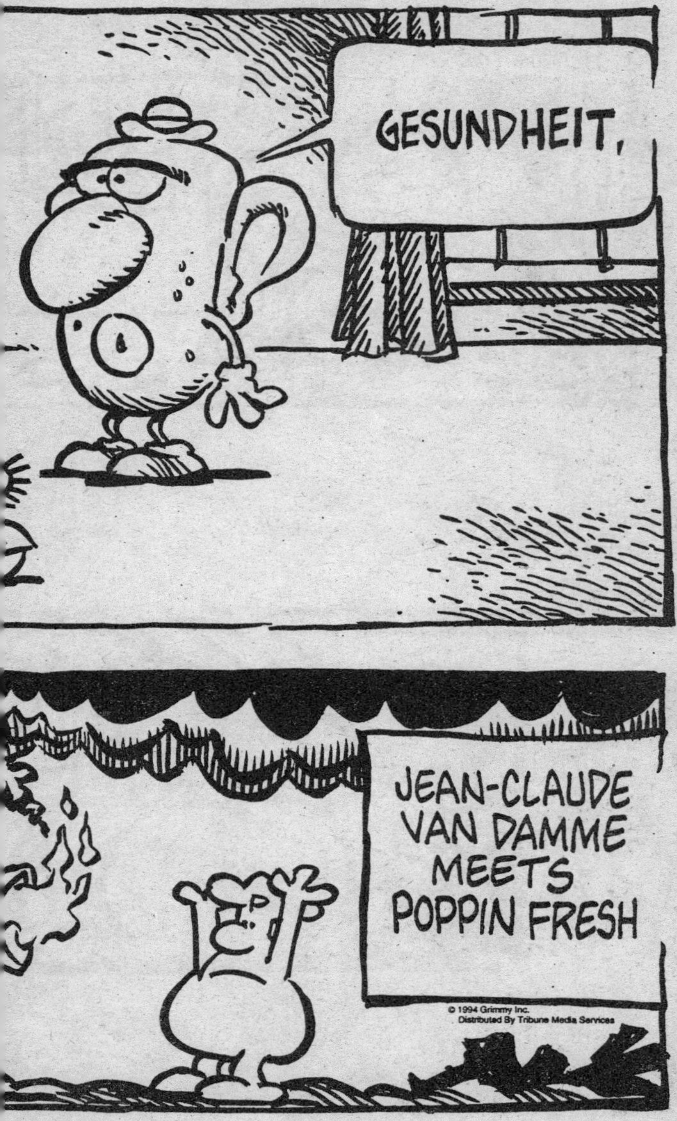
GESUNDHEIT,
JEAN-CLAUDE VAN DAMME MEETS POPPIN FRESH
© 1994 Grimmy Inc.
Distributed By Tribune Media Services

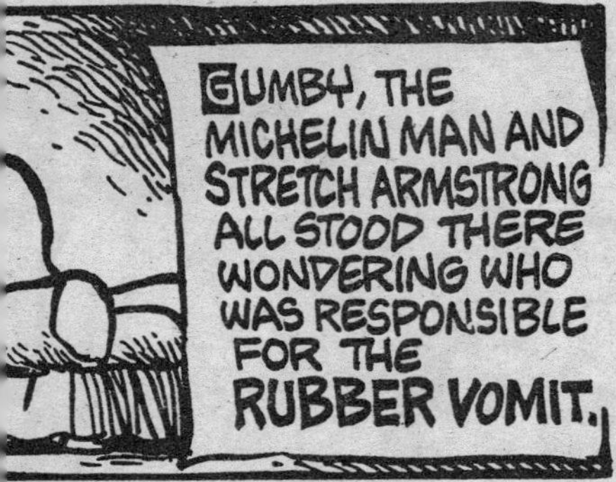
GUMBY, THE MICHELIN MAN AND STRETCH ARMSTRONG ALL STOOD THERE WONDERING WHO WAS RESPONSIBLE FOR THE RUBBER VOMIT.

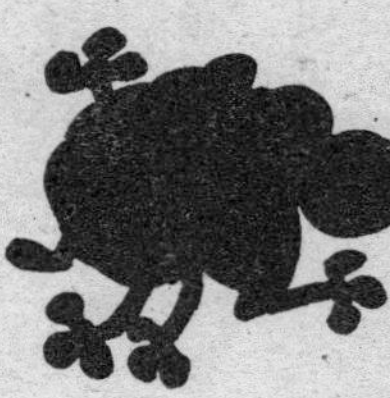

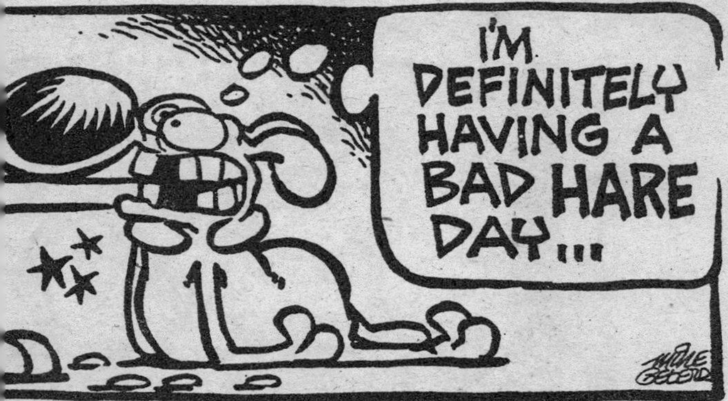
I'M DEFINITELY HAVING A BAD HARE DAY...

GIFT RETURNS
3/30

3-15

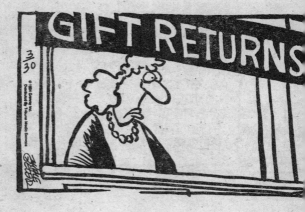

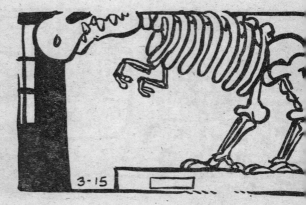

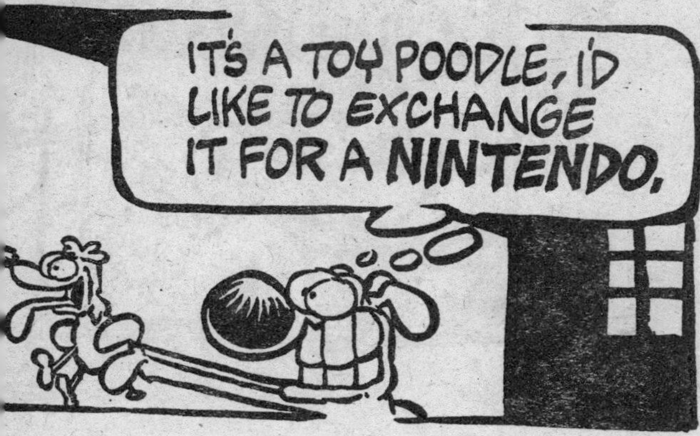
IT'S A TOY POODLE, I'D LIKE TO EXCHANGE IT FOR A NINTENDO.

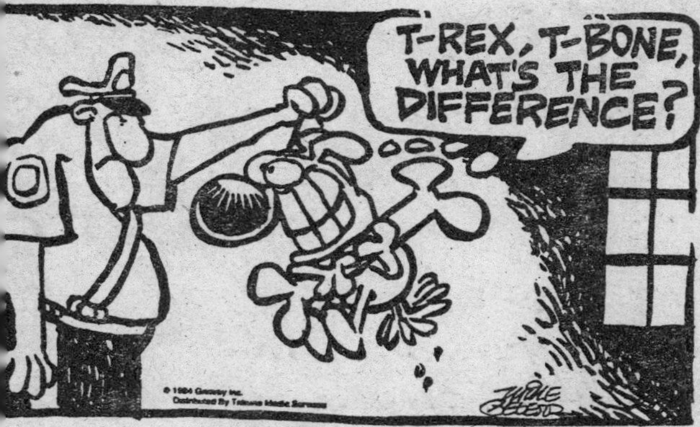
T-REX, T-BONE, WHAT'S THE DIFFERENCE?

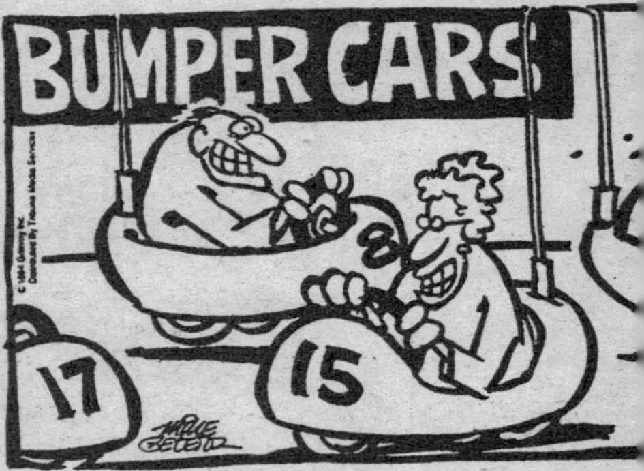
BUMPER CARS
© 1994 Grimmy Inc.
Distributed By Tribune Media Services
17
15

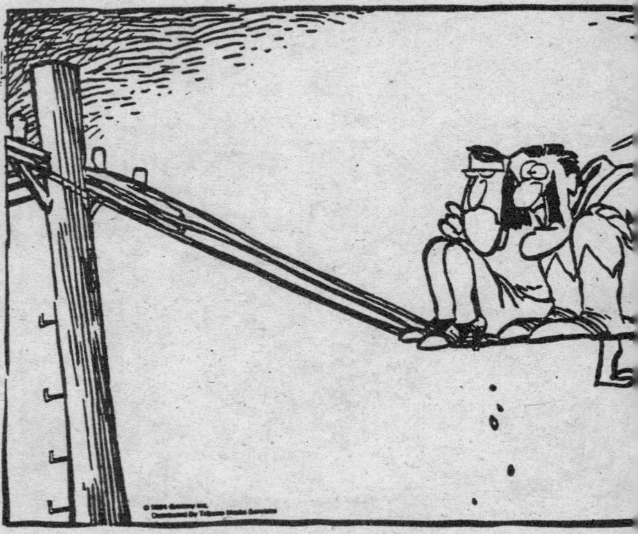

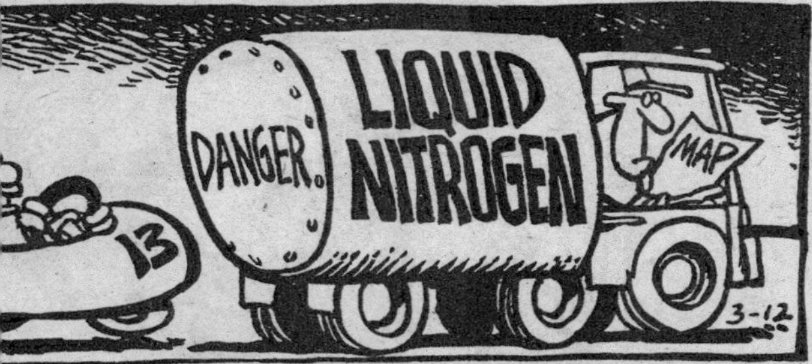
DANGER.
LIQUID NITROGEN
MAP
13
3-12

ERB HAD A PERFECT SAFETY RECORD EXCEPT
OR ONE UNFORTUNATE WRONG TURN...

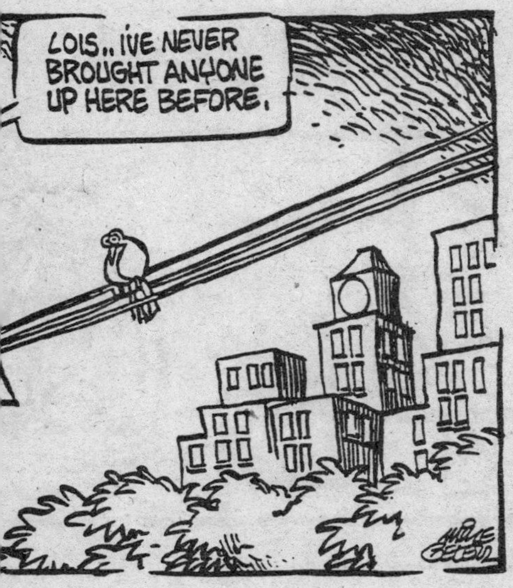
LOIS.. I'VE NEVER BROUGHT ANYONE UP HERE BEFORE.

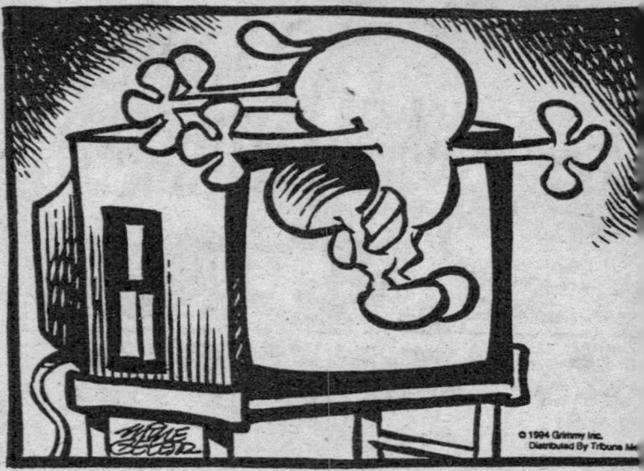
© 1994 Grimmy Inc.
Distributed By Tribune Me

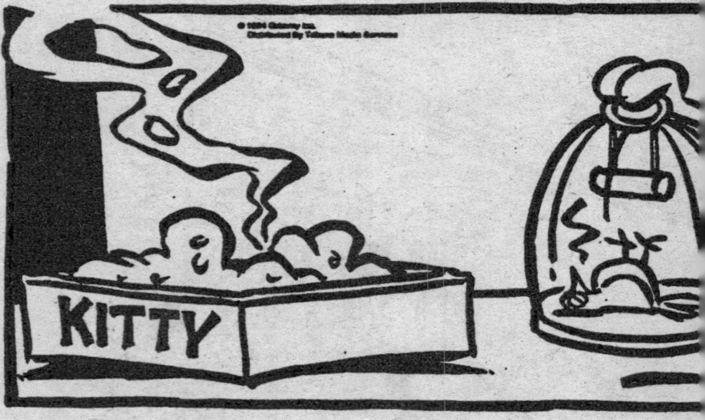
KITTY

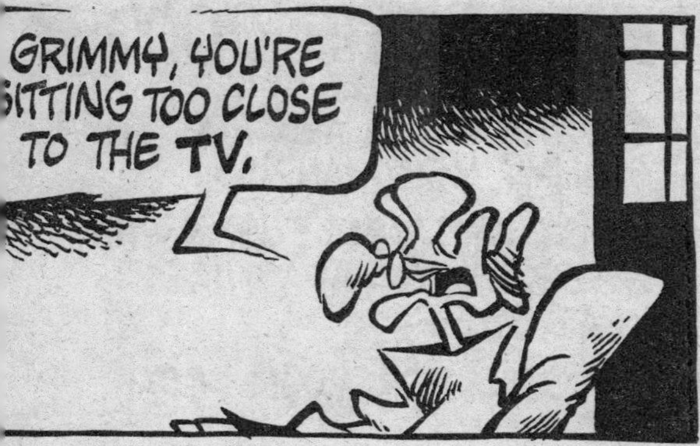
GRIMMY, YOU'RE SITTING TOO CLOSE TO THE TV.

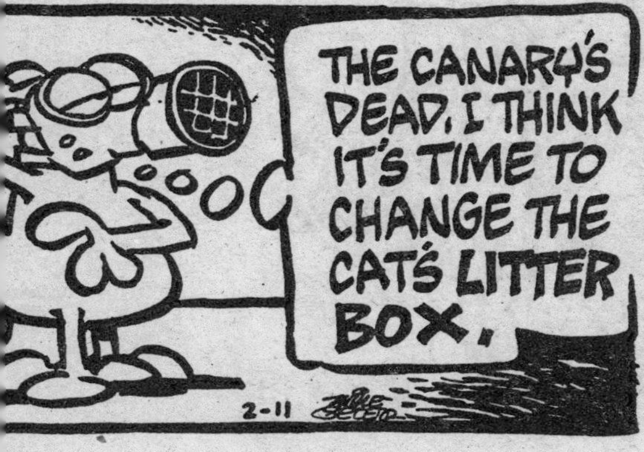
THE CANARY'S DEAD. I THINK IT'S TIME TO CHANGE THE CAT'S LITTER BOX.
2-11

# WHERE ARE THE GOODS?

MANY OF OUR READERS ASK HOW THEY CAN BUY GRIMMY MERCHANDISE.

HERE IS A LIST OF LICENSEES IN THE UNITED STATES AND CANADA THAT CARRY GREAT STUFF!

GIVE THEM A CALL FOR YOUR LOCAL DISTRIBUTOR.

WWW.GRIMMY.COM

**The Antioch Company**
888 Dayton St.
Yellow Springs, OH 45387

PH 800/543-2397
Bookmarks, Wallet Cards,
"Largely Literary" products:
T-Shirts, Mugs, Journals, Pens,
Notepads, Bookplates, Bookmarks

**Avalanche Publishing**
1093 Bedmar St.
Carson, CA 90746

PH 310/223-1600
365 Day Box Calendar-Year 2000
www.avalanchepub.com

**Classcom, Inc.**
770 Bertrand
Montreal, Quebec
Canada H4M1V9

PH 514/747-9492
Desk Art

**C.T.I.**
22160 North Pepper Rd.
Barrington, IL 60010

PH 800/284-5605
Balloons, Coffee Mugs

**F.X. Schmid/USA**
1 Puzzle Lane
Newton, NH 03858

PH 800/886-1236
Puzzles
www.fxschmid.com

**Gibson Greetings**
2100 Section Rd.
Cincinnati, OH 45237

PH 800/345-6521
Greeting Cards, Party
Papers, Gift Wrap etc...
www.greetst.com

**Linda Jones Enterprises**
17771 Mitchell
Irvine, CA 92614

PH 949/660-7791
Cels

**MR. TEES**
3225 Hartsfield Rd.
Tallahassee, FL 32303

PH 850/574-3737
T-Shirts

**Pomegranate**
210 Classic Ct.
Rohnert Park, CA 94928

PH 800/227-1428
Wall Year 2000 Calendars,
Postcard Booklets
www.pomegranate.com

**Second Nature Software**
1325 Officers' Row
Vancouver, WA 98661

PH 360/737-4170
Screen Saver Program
www.secondnature.com

**TOR Books**
175 Fifth Ave.
New York, NY 10010

PH 212/388-0100
Paperback Books
www.tor.com

**Western Graphics**
3535 W. 1st Avenue
Eugene, OR 97402

PH 800/532-3303
Posters